Swarm Intelligence and Its Applications in Biomedical Informatics

Swarm Intelligence and Its Applications in Biomedical Informatics discusses Artificial Intelligence (AI) applications in medicine and biology, as well as challenges and opportunities presented in these arenas. It covers healthcare big data analytics, mobile health, personalized medicine, and clinical trial data management. This book shows how AI can be used for early disease diagnosis, prediction, and prognosis, and it offers healthcare case studies that demonstrate the application of AI and Machine Learning.

Key Features:

- Covers all major topics of swarm intelligence research and development such as novel-based search methods and novel optimization algorithm: applications of swarm intelligence to management problems and swarm intelligence for real-world application.
- Provides a unique insight into the complex problems of bioinformatics and the innovative solutions which make up 'intelligent bioinformatics'.
- Covers a wide range of topics on the role of AI, Machine Learning, and Big Data for healthcare applications and deals with the ethical issues and concerns associated with it.
- Explores applications in different areas of healthcare and highlights the current research.

This book is designed as a reference text, and it aims primarily at advanced undergraduates and postgraduate students studying computer science and bioinformatics. Researchers and professionals will find this book useful.

A. Sheik Abdullah is an Assistant Professor senior, at the School of Computer Science Engineering, Vellore Institute of Technology, in Chennai, Tamil Nadu, India. His research interests include Medical Data Research and Analytics, E-Governance, and Big Data. He has published books, written book chapters, and numerous journal articles.

Swarm Intelligence and Its Applications in Biomedical Informatics

Dr. A. Sheik Abdullah

CRC Press
Taylor & Francis Group
Boca Raton London New York

CRC Press is an imprint of the
Taylor & Francis Group, an **informa** business

First edition published 2024
by CRC Press
2385 NW Executive Center Drive, Suite 320, Boca Raton FL 33431

and by CRC Press
4 Park Square, Milton Park, Abingdon, Oxon, OX14 4RN

CRC Press is an imprint of Taylor & Francis Group, LLC

ISBN: 978-1-032-35649-5 (hbk)
ISBN: 978-1-032-36090-4 (pbk)
ISBN: 978-1-003-33018-9 (ebk)

DOI: 10.1201/9781003330189

Typeset in Times
by codeMantra

To my wonderful wife R Kaja Nisha and my son AS Arfan.

*To my Brother A Mohammed Nazeem and
my sister A Noorul Mufina Begum.*

To my parents and parents-in-law.

Contents

Preface

Companies and educational institutions are conceptualizing rapid change in technology and societal patterns due to high interconnectivity and intelligent automation systems. It enhances the boundaries between the physical, digital, and biological worlds. Significant advances in biological sciences with the acceleration toward the development of computing, data analysis, and interpretation are making the environment diverse in computational biology. As a part of this, nature-inspired computing is raising its hands to learn and automate from the environmental states and happenings to formulate decision-making for real-time analysis. Some computational processes include swarm intelligence, artificial immune system, and amorphous computing.

This book is written in a focused way because it is targeted toward health informatics. A reader's prerequisite knowledge should include some essential exposure to data analysis, data classification, statistical modeling, swarm intelligence, feature selection, and visual data exploration. This book includes examples of real-time case studies which correspond to non-communicable diseases. The author has integrated both his research and experience through various chapters. This book is aimed at medical data analytics, analytics practitioners, faculty members, and Ph.D. researchers starting to explore the field.

To my wonderful wife R Kaja Nisha and my son AS Arfan.

To my Brother A Mohammed Nazeem and my sister A Noorul Mufina Begum.

1 Introduction

1.1 BACKGROUND OF BIOMEDICAL INFORMATICS

The domain of medical informatics is concerned with the knowledge of information and computer science, engineering, and technology for health studies, medicine, and its practices [1]. Medical informatics has progressed for the past 30 years as healthcare tried to explore complex information through functional patterns and data generated by computer systems. The evolution of research was initiated in medical informatics in the 1950s to explore new findings, risk behaviors, and the likelihood of disease-specific syndromes [2]. Figure 1.1 depicts the classification of biomedical informatics and its functionalities.

1.1.1 METHODS IN BIOMEDICAL INFORMATICS

Biomedical informatics has three significant components in classifying the data intended to develop the decision support model. Risk analysis and disease prediction in bioinformatics include the applicability of computational techniques to formulate their goal. Informatics techniques such as statistics, machine learning, soft computing, swarm intelligence, data mining, and data visualization have been used in medical data. Hence, computational and statistical methods are used to determine the aspects of a specified disease. Bioinformatics can be broadly classified into three types based on the data type to be processed to frame the decision support model. They are bioinformatics, imaging informatics, and public health informatics. The process behind biomedical informatics includes data analysis and data interpretation, which are considered the significant tasks in risk determination.

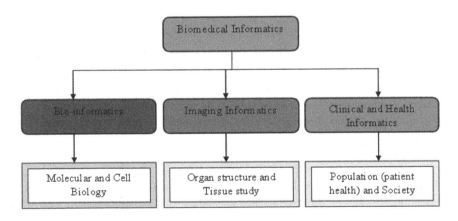

FIGURE 1.1 Classification in biomedical informatics.

DOI: 10.1201/9781003330189-1

1.1.1.1 Bioinformatics

The platform of bioinformatics includes determining aspects related to gene structure, anticipated properties of diseases, and nucleotide polymorphism structure. The structure provides the determination of disease syndromes with its attribute properties. The protein sequence and its properties can be located by the disease specified. The sequential structure of proteins and the organizational structure of nucleic acids can be clearly understood with the processing paradigms and incorporations over bioinformatics. The field of bioinformatics includes processing a large variety of data based on the type and the nature of informatics. It entails the development of algorithms to detect gene structure and its sequence to predict the nature of protein structure and its function-related sequences.

The primary goal behind bioinformatics is to regulate the realization of the biological process. Over the decades, bioinformatics has had its rapid growth over the technological developments in molecular biology. Common research interest in bioinformatics includes analyzing and designing deoxyribonucleic acid (DNA) sequences, protein sequences, and protein structures with three-dimensional modeling [3].

1.1.1.2 Imaging Informatics

Imaging science informatics incorporates the usage of Information and Communication Technology (ICT) to manipulate, handle, and analyze image data [4]. Imaging science aims to improve the utilization and services that render medical imaging and healthcare technology. The disciplines in imaging sciences include orthopedics, cardiology, obstetrics and gynecology, surgery in general medicine, and pathology. The department of imaging science is fundamentally the one among a data-technology-driven field of professionals in medicine radiology which has been assigned the role of the front-runners in imaging informatics.

The domain of imaging informatics provides various facilitations at the interface of information, computer science, and biological sciences. It aids the computer-assisted way of medical diagnosis along with the clinical services by incorporating technological methods into the decision-making process. It also serves as the mechanism for managing medical equipment, which is an essential tool in life-saving post-operation surgeries.

1.1.1.3 Clinical and Public Health Informatics (Health Informatics)

Health informatics deals with computer science, information science, and healthcare. It provides enhancements over methods, resources, and services to enhance data acquisition, processing, optimization, and retrieval. This multi-disciplinary system helps make proper decisions concerning the parameters of healthcare technology with the target of decision-making.

Current technological research in medical science targets the developmental processes and tools for preventing diseases and syndromes [5]. Every country has adopted control measures to determine the root cause and risk factors corresponding to specific diseases. In considering the perspective of research and technology over disease prediction, advancement in medical devices and facilitation and decision support model could pave the right path for rescuing the society from the disease.

Better realization and interventions in healthcare informatics are needed to reduce the impact of communicable and non-communicable diseases [6].

1.2 MEDICAL ASPECTS OF COMMUNICABLE AND NON-COMMUNICABLE DISEASES

The report on communicable and non-communicable diseases, as per the World Health Organization (WHO), states that it has been the leading cause of death that targets morbidity and mortality in developing countries [7]. The southeast Asian region has a high probability of communicable diseases. It has failed to destroy diseases that are preventable through vaccine insemination. Hence, the present global economic condition is severely affected by these emerging diseases that can increase daily death rates. The international agencies and collaborators join hands to raise the treatment, preventive measures, and control of communicable diseases by various means of communication [8].

Non-communicable diseases (NCDs) are considered the central problem in India, which accounts for 62% of total disability-adjusted life years and 53% of total deaths [9]. The projection of NCD is mainly due to the socio-economic conditions and the risk factors that contribute to the disease. Research studies in India show that 25% of people are affected by cardiovascular disease (CVD) and 50% with cancer. The incurring expenses for hospitalization were about 160% and higher for NCD. The rate of percentage for NCD has moved to a diverse range of 22%–35% and 32%–40% in the years from 1995 to 2004.

The increase in NCD is typically due to the clinical interventions, dietary habits, and the locality of the people. The risk factors of the disease may specifically range from one level to another by the nature of living. Meanwhile, clinical expenses should also be considered a factor in over-diagnosis of NCD.

The health sector needs to be improved by enhancing medical facilities, determining disease-specific risk factor, and spreading health awareness. In addition to the health sector, there lies an individual responsibility and awareness specific to the disease. Enhancing and rendering health-based services also depend upon the likelihood and habits of the people around a specific region. If the risk-specific syndromes are detected in advance, the cost-effectiveness and treatment expenses can be avoided, thereby allowing us to render a population-based healthcare service.

The burden of disease statistics with the ratio survey in 2012 conveyed that the birth rate for males and females increased by 5 years compared to the WHO region average. In 2012, the realm of health expectancy in males and females was 9 years lower than that of birth expectancy. Hence, the rate of loss in life expectancy is due to the loss of disability in the population. Table 1.1 provides the rate of NCD mortality with its specific metabolic and behavioral risk factors.

As per the statistical report from the WHO, the death rate for cardiovascular disease and diabetes is high compared to other NCDs. The report also suggests that metabolic and behavioral risk factors play a vital role in NCD deaths. The WHO states that NCD affects about 40 million people per year, contributing to an overall progression of about 70% of deaths. When considering the age-group-based analysis,

TABLE 1.1

Estimation of NCD Deaths Statistical Report from the WHO

NCD Mortality	Males	Females
Total NCD deaths	2,968	2,274
NCD deaths under the age of 60	38	32
Death rate per 1,00,000		
All NCD	781.7	571.0
Cancers	78.8	71.8
Chronic respiratory disease	178.4	125.5
Cardiovascular disease and diabetes	386.3	263.0

over 15 million people die in the age group 30–69, with 80% of premature deaths mostly happening in low- and middle-income-based countries as per Global Burden of Disease (GBD) statistics (GBD Risk Factors Collaborators 2016). Among the death rate, CVD (stroke and heart problems) accounts for about 17.7 million deaths, cancers 8.8 million, respiratory problems (pulmonary disease and asthma) 3.9 million, and diabetes for about 1.6 million. Detection of the disease based upon risk factors (modifiable and non-modifiable) can act as a preventive measure, overcoming medicinal impacts and their complications.

Risk factors include modifiable and non-modifiable features, specifically for each disease. Some of the factors may rise due to physical activities, use of alcohol, tobacco, dietary habits, and mainly urbanization. People with irregular diets and physical activities may have increased glucose levels, blood pressures, and lipid levels. These risk factors are the metabolic factors that can lead to CVD.

1.2.1 STATISTICAL REPORT FOR RISK FACTORS OF NCD

The behavioral risk factors include unhealthy diet, alcohol, tobacco, and physical inactivity. The death corresponding to utilization of tobacco accounts for about 7.2 million per year, which seems to increase over the years. Moreover, 3.3 million deaths have been owing to the usage of alcohol for NCD and cancer. The distribution and consumption of alcohol-specific drugs has been increasing. It has also been reported that 1.6 million deaths are due to physical inactivity and 4.1 million deaths due to the increased usage of salt and sodium in dietary habits. Due to urbanization, in many of the regions, the lifestyle, dietary habits, and the way of living have made the people adhere to the living conditions which again are the root cause for the increase in diseases and deaths.

Regarding metabolic risk factors, about 19% of deaths have been recorded as contributing toward blood pressure levels, glucose levels (hyperglycemia), obesity, and increased levels of fat in blood. These factors are the key measures that highly contribute toward NCD. The strategy of NCD interference is needed for the target reduction of about 25% in risk that contributes toward the disease. The WHO has set a target of one-third reduction of the disease by 2030. If the risk is determined in accordance with regions, then the problem of cost expensive treatment can be solved in advance.

1.2.2 EPIDEMIOLOGY OF NON-COMMUNICABLE DISEASE

NCDs, which are also called chronic disease, are not transferred from one person to another. They generally make very slow progression among the infected persons over time. These diseases probably rise due to premature dysfunction and morbidity levels from the initial stages of birth or due to the quality of living. The term epidemiology specifically relates to the determination of causes and spread of disease-specific factors among particular group of people to control health issues and the related problems. Hence, the key factors that contribute to the disease among the specified group of people can be discerned to solve health problems. The term epidemiology deals with the following cases:

1. Disease distribution
2. Determining factor
3. Health-affected regions
4. Specific work group/Population

The impact and occurrence of disease across specific groups of people play a significant role in most of the developing countries. If epidemiological factors are known in advance, the effect of disease and its risk factors can be known early enough to have a region-based analysis.

1.2.3 PURPOSE OF EPIDEMIOLOGICAL STUDY AND ASSUMPTIONS

Epidemiological study is mainly concerned with the analysis, occurrence, and distribution of demographics of disease statistics for the specified region or country. The elements such as behavioral, social, and biological factors over the rate of distribution of the disease can be found accordingly from the statistical measures as per demography. The following distributions describe the purpose of epidemiological learning:

1. To quantify the frequency of the disease.
2. To measure the distribution of the disease.
3. To determine the determinants of the disease such as the risk factors corresponding to social, behavioral, physical, and biological risk factors.
4. To formulate the hypothesis corresponding to the cause, effects, and its preventive measures for developing a decision support model.

As an outcome of the study, the realm of person being affected by the disease when it occurs and where it happens can be found out and tested accordingly. The testing factor serves as the model for the determination of the risk factors that contribute to the disease. Hence, a decision support framework can be modeled in accordance with the disease-specific syndromes.

1.3   BIOMEDICAL INFORMATICS

The domain of biomedical informatics utilizes different variants of data in different formats to represent the distinguishable patterns. The evolved patterns include clinical insights, disease recovery, treatment analysis, and the scientific facts that have been revealed as a part of diagnostic analysis. Some of the most notable examples include clinical warehouse, clinical research models, Electronic Health Records (EHR) response patterns, and clinical decision support systems.

1.3.1   IT-ORIENTED DEFINITIONS

The term biomedical informatics is considered to be one of the branches of healthcare informatics which enables the healthcare practitioners and researchers to adapt 'Technology for Healthcare'. The biomedical informatics is not solely tied up with technology, but it depends on technology-driven, healthcare-enabled service with the dependency toward artificial intelligence, robotics, decision support models, and digitization of personal healthcare services. It should also be noted that significant cloud-based storage with secure data transmission is involved to regularly track the variation in genomics and DNA transformation patterns. Similar practice is also followed to determine the notable patterns of varying diseases using wearable devices with the aid in support toward imaging, visualization, and data analysis.

1.3.2   COMPUTATION – A TOOL FOR INFORMATICS

The impact of problem solving in providing solutions depends on the type of the application that we consider for evaluation. Problem solving in technology includes a step-by-step procedure which includes the mechanism of

- Identifying the problem
- Formalizing the problem
- Developing an algorithm/procedure which has the ability to solve the problem
- Testing and validating the problem with significant codes

Data computation is carried out in accordance with the problem-solving strategy and its intermediate process. Biomedical computation merges the mechanism of problem-solving tools of technology with the advancement in life sciences which then results in the possible ways to improve healthcare practice. As the data is growing abundantly from time to time, the need for the demand in processing tools has been increased rapidly [10]. In order to overcome and address this problem, different computation tools in healthcare technology aid in data processing, model development along with interpretation and justification. UpToDate, Virgin Pulse, Cerner care tracker, Vizient, HealApp, and PatientIQ are examples of computational tools. When concerning about the type of the data used in medical domain, the processing varies in accordance to the format and size of utilization. Significant data analytics and statistical tools are used in biomedical informatics for developing models and deriving conclusions. Some of them are Stata, R, GraphPad Prism, SAS, SPSS, Matlab, JMP, Minitab, and Statistica [11].

1.3.3 Benefits and Applications of Biomedical Informatics

Biomedical informatics provides an utmost protection and enhancement toward the patient care and life sciences discipline. The mechanism of data collection, storage, and analysis along with the clinical information is important in executing day-to-day activities of the healthcare organizations. The process of requirement analysis and the jobs/tasks assigned to the medical experts vary with respect to time and the nature of process assigned [12]. Much of the benefits of biomedical informatics include reduced service costs, improved productivity, improvised QoS (Quality of Service), and strategic regulatory considerations. During clinical trials and measurements, the safety and testing of pharmacovigilance programs significant predictive analytics is made with regard to the determination of errors and process issues.

One of the great challenges toward healthcare informatics is the changes adopted in Management Information System (MIS). Significant investments have been made by government organizations and healthcare authorities in order to render the notable needs and factors that contribute toward different diseases [13].

1.3.4 Structural Bioinformatics and Proteome-Based Technology

The domain of structural bioinformatics relates to the category of bioinformatics which completely deals with the prediction and analysis of three-dimensional variant structure of biological macromolecules. This involves the components such as proteins, ribonucleic acid (RNA), and DNA. The process includes generalizations with the three-dimensional structure which includes comparison among folds, molecular folding, binding interactions, structural relationships, and deriving computational models. The term 'structural' has the same meaning in structural bioinformatics and structural biology, both of which are parts of computational biology.

Meanwhile in genomics, the studies are anticipated with the determination of genome structure and its biological aspects. In general, comparative genomics is the process behind signature selection to represent the evolutionary process that occurs on genomes. This is still an active research arena which determines the species evolution and species determination. The information that is being present in modern genomes signifies the automation of gene finding and functional determination. Different forms of computation strategies have been evolved to signify the nature and aspects of genomic study in bioinformatics analysis. Collective inferences on public cases have proven the strategy of genomic comparison and expression analysis. This in turn increased system analysis, coding information, string matching, and the generation of decision support models.

1.3.5 Bio-programming and Bioinformatics Software

The software that are meant for bio-programming and bioinformatics are designed for sequence and structural analysis for biological databases. Significant factors need to be considered during the evaluation stages of programming and analysis based on the type of data to be used. In order to meet the requirements of the user and the need to retrieve data based on the requests, the use of tool may vary. Some of the software are available in standard version and some other in customized version. For the second category, the user may alter the output format based on their needs and visual perceptions. The categorization of the tools used in bioinformatics includes similarity analysis tools, protein function analysis, and structural analysis (Table 1.2).

The domain of ICT plays a significant role in the evaluation of data which falls under different categories and types. The realm of data processing lies at the way of understanding the basic constructs and making the right tool for analysis.

1.3.6 Disease Patterns and Treatment Analysis

The existence of disease and its syndromes occurs in different ways based on the level of occurrence, risk factors, and most importantly, the location, likelihood, and dietary habits of the people. Over the past years, much importance has been given to the study of disease origin, pattern of establishment and its associations. Each of the healthcare organizations is operating with regard to the establishment of determining the comorbidities and the significant outcomes that focus toward the clinical management service. The term comorbidity refers to the co-occurrence of two or more

TABLE 1.2
List of Bioinformatics Software

Name of the Software	Applications and Usage
ALLPATHS-LG	It corresponds to the evaluation of mammalian-sized genomes
Bedtools	It corresponds to the evaluation of intersecting, merging, and complimenting the genomic intervals across multiple files
Bioconductor	It provides the analysis of high-scaled genomic data along with R programming
Boost	It enhances a fast approach in detecting gene to gene interactions which suitably happens in case control studies
ClustalW	It generates multi-sequence program to align and reframe the DNA as well as protein sequences
Gnuplot	It is an interactive command-driven plotting program
iSAAC	It corresponds to the DNA sequence aligner with high memory utilization
Matplotlib	A generic plotting mechanism and an library function in python programming (extension NumPy)
Python	It is a high-level, interpretive, and multi-purpose programming language
R	It is a programming language for statistical analysis and graphical interpretation
SQLite	It is a database engine supported with a family of embedded databases
variant_tools	It is a complete set of tools for investigating annotation, manipulation, and simulation analysis of variants

disease conditions for a specified time period. The impact may rise to reduced life quality, increased cost, and high rate of mortality conditions.

In recent days, the use of EHR is maintained and managed by all the medical institutions in order to overcome the delay in retrieving the health information and the medical history related to the patients. At certain stages, the scenario of population-based health analysis is also made through EHR to specifically measure the risk factors that tend to spread the communicable or non-communicable disease toward region-based analysis. However, time-based analysis is used for determining the risk that is associated with communicable diseases. This measure quantifies the complete data-driven evaluation pattern for determining the disease-specific syndromes associated with the disease [14].

Major form of associated comorbidities includes historical reviews, complex patterns, disease progression with time, early diagnosis, and potentially harmful defects. Different forms of variants exist among the patient's group to represent the varying patterns among the same disease-specific syndromes. But the notable thing is to identify the relationship among the patterns that diverge from the disease. At certain point of analysis, the resultant risk factor may tend to the evolution of other such diseases in general. This should be noted with regard to the time and origin of the disease with regard to location, likelihood and dietary habits of the people.

1.3.7 SCIENTIFIC DEMAND ANALYSIS AND OUTCOMES

Information is determined to be the key asset for any organization to rationalize its development. The more information we have, the more possible scenarios there are for notable deliverables to have best outcomes and values. Hence, at all stages, the realm of data collection is considered to be an important feature for processing, estimation, analysis, and decision-making process. If the data corresponding to the specified domain is formatted accordingly, then it can be easily used for analysis for good decision-making at intermediate levels. Due to the massive increase in data records in each sector, the technological advancements for storing these abundant forms of data have to be upgraded. In order to represent this scenario, the term 'big data' has been evolved with notable parameters [15]. To fulfill the needs and to retrieve and analyze the data at right time, the healthcare industry has to adapt to technological incorporations and future prospects of big data.

The healthcare sector generates different formats of big data in terms of HER, medical records, examination results, prescriptions from time to time, and data that has been generated from medical devices. Research in biomedical health informatics requires proper data management facility to solve different kinds of issues such as patient related issues, medical related issues, and doctors' suggestions, as well as the associated challenges and high-end computing solutions associated with big data.

Upon considering data management, analysis, and monitoring, the modern healthcare technology can change its perspective to the new era of ICT with big data. Also, the domain is taking its inception by introducing robots, Internet of Things (IOT), and Artificial Intelligence (AI) in clinical informatics to accomplish complex vigorous tasks to afford best service in time. This in turn executes different forms of personalized healthcare service with automated environment in medical services.

1.3.8 APPLICATIONS

Automated application in clinical informatics is deployed in a variety of self-care services for remote patient monitoring and analysis. IOT sensor-based devices are involved with healthcare services like glucose monitoring, heart rate monitoring, depression status analysis, and Parkinson's disease analysis. Online treatment analysis has been increased in recent days, cases pertaining to asthma or COPD which influences with warning status on the attack pertaining to the disease. At certain situations, connected inhalers are used to determine the risk of patients suffering with attack, allowing it to be easily determined if they are prone to the disease.

Ingestible sensors play a significant role in collecting data inside the human body particularly at digestive systems and their components to measure the pH levels and discover internal bleeding. Some of the sensors can be swallowed, and some are fixed at specific locations to efficiently monitor the human actions and defect conditions. Similarly, smart contact lenses provide an automated way of passively collecting healthcare information. This smart lens includes micro cameras which spontaneously capture eye information like Google innovation in connected contact lenses.

Robots enrolled with AI play a significant role in clinical informatics and its applications. Some of the major incorporation of robots involves the usage of internet connected robots inside the human body to perform complex surgical process and to stop disease mutations. Similarly, significant robotic surgeries are performed along with the inclusion of IOT devices for faster and accurate surgical analysis.

The major challenge with regard to these applications is the device design and fitting with human body. Different people respond differently for the devices that are ingested into the human body. The data transfer and adequacy of data from the device to the digital components has to be addressed carefully. Also, the set of qualified device standards and its components need to be monitored 24×7 for efficient handling of medical devices. In recent days, different forms of attacks are happening in stealing device-dependent medical data. A total of about 82% of the healthcare sector raised a dispute against the attacks that have happened in lieu of attacking the medical devices ingested in human body [16]. This should be analyzed with proper security measures through the government and its policy guidelines along with the Indian Medical Association (IMA). If the measures are properly identified with significant classification of threats and attacks, then the risk level can be reduced. The vulnerabilities and the anomalies can thus be sorted out with explicit classification and regulation of device management in the healthcare sector [17].

1.4 APPLICATION OF BIG DATA IN BIOMEDICAL INFORMATICS

Quite simply, the big data era is in full force today as the world is changing through instrumentation. We are clever to sense more objects, and if we can sense it, we tend to try and store it. Through advances in communications technology, people and things are becoming increasingly connected – not just some of the time, but all of the time. This intersecting rate is an escape train. Generally referred to as machine-to-machine (M2M), interconnectivity is responsible for double-digit year-over-year data growth rates. Finally, because small integrated circuits are now so cheap, we are able to add intelligence to almost everything [18].

1.4.1 BIG DATA – AN INTRODUCTION

An organization generates and manages a large amount of volume data, which makes big data analytics tools to be the most important tool in enterprises. The big data analytics tool should be expanded when analyzing data cleaning, data mining, data duplicates, and data visualization. Big data does not change only in predictive analysis but also changes our power of thinking and knowledge. These techniques are used in quickly analyzing the real-time organizations and industries' dataset. These technologies change the world's business and also help in good decision-making [19]. This is an emerging technology for companies and it has been applied to analyze big data analytics in cloud, Hadoop, deep learning, and no SQL and in-memory analytics. Banking and securities, communications and media, healthcare, education, insurance, consumer trade, and transportation are the top sectors used by big data analytics. For example, the global spread of the Ebola virus strains has been identified in different countries using a data analytics tool. The collected datasets and subsequently surveys were used in the research. For the datasets to be analyzed accurately, experts have to apply some skills like programming, data warehousing, computational frameworks, quantitative aptitude and statistics, and business knowledge. The predictive analytics is a perfect analytics process in the current state that defines the correlation and source for obtaining the quality of data. In the process, IT and digital agencies are involved in applying different types of tools. These tools are recognized when solving various dataset issues such as determining whether the right data will be enough for a system. Identifying big data solutions for data processing recommends using the popular open source. Tools include Apache Hadoop, Apache Spark, Apache Strom, Apache Cassandra, Mango Db, R programming Environment, Neo4j, and Apache SAMOA. However, there are many big data analytics tools available in recent years [20].

1.4.2 THE FOUR VS OF BIG DATA

Big data analytics are processed in varied datasets. An organization generates and manages a large amount of volume data, making big data analytics tools the most important tool in enterprises. The big data analytics tool should be expanded when analyzing data cleaning, data mining, data duplicates, and data visualization. Big data does not change only in predictive analysis but also changes our power of thinking and knowledge.

These techniques are used in quickly analyzing the real-time organizations and industries' dataset. These technologies change the world's business and also help in good decision-making. This is an emerging technology for companies that has been applied to analyze big data analytics in the cloud, Hadoop, deep learning, and no SQL and in-memory analytics. Banking and securities, communications and media, healthcare, education, insurance, consumer trade, and transportation are the top sectors used by big data analytics [21].

Big data solution for the data processing recommends using the popular open source. Tools such as Apache Hadoop, Apache Spark, Apache Strom, Apache Cassandra, Mango Db, R programming Environment, Neo4j, and Apache SAMOA are used. There are many big data analytics tools available in recent years, but the next generation of mobile app will use the current demographics [22]. These data analytics tools are R programming, Weka, and rapid miner.

Big data is generally defined by four Vs such as:

- Volume
- Velocity
- Variety
- Veracity

The volume corresponds to the amount of data that is being created from time to time. The size of the data may vary from some gigabytes to terabytes to petabytes. In all the real-time applications, the quantity of the data is considered to be an important feature to deal with new technology and its strategies for data storage and analysis.

The second factor corresponds to velocity, which in turn relates to the speed of the data generated from time to time. Applications focusing on real-time data such as Facebook, Twitter, and Instagram create data tremendously with greater speed and the same is processed within the stipulated time. This factor is considered to be the key attribute of big data in all data processing platforms.

Different forms of data need different types of processing platforms with different technologies. The way in which the data gets formulated has its key characteristic to get processed. This third factor variety corresponds to the data specifically available in different formats such as text, images, log files, audio/video, database, and other unstructured or semi-structured formats. The technology and its paradigms involved in processing those unstructured big data are considered to be the challenging task that was not possible during the past days [23].

The fourth factor veracity of big data corresponds to the trustworthiness. It explicitly corresponds to the accuracy and quality of the data that is to be used up for analysis. Even if the data comes from different forms of data sources, it is much more important to derive the meaningful patterns only if the data is of high quality and has good accuracy as a factor. In order to optimize the business process for good and understandable decision-making, it is necessary to have valid methods for data analysis and process even it is of varying sizes and formats.

1.4.3 Importance of Big Data in Clinical Informatics

Big data technologies are progressively used more for biomedical and healthcare informatics research. Large amounts of biological and clinical data have been generated and collected at an exceptional speed and scale. A number of scenarios in healthcare are well suited for a big data solution. In 2001, Doug Laney, now at Gartner, coined the term 'the 3 Vs' to define big data – Volume, Velocity, and Variety. Other analysts have argued that this is too simplistic, and that there are more things to think about when defining big data. They suggest more Vs, such as Variability and Veracity, and even a C for Complexity. Modern years have seen an escalating volume of medical image data and observations being gathered and accumulated. Collaborative, global ideas have begun the acquisition of hundreds of terabytes/petabytes of data to be made accessible to the medical and scientific community. For example, the new generation of sequencing technologies enables the dispensation of billions of DNA sequence data per day, while the application of EHRs is documenting large amounts of patient data. Handling out these large datasets and processing is a challenging task. Together with the new medical opportunities arising, new image and data processing algorithms are required for functioning with, and learning from, large-scale medical datasets [24].

'Big Data' is a key word in the medical and healthcare sector for patient care. NASA researchers coined the term big data in 1967 to describe the huge amount of information being generated by supercomputers. It has evolved to include all data streaming from various sources – cell phones, mobile devices, Satellites, Google, Amazon, and Twitter. The impact of big data may be deep, and it will have in-depth implications for medical imaging as healthcare tracks, handles, exploits, and documents relevant patient information. Medical data collection can necessitate an incredible amount of time and effort once collected; the information can be utilized in several ways:

- To improve early detection, diagnosis, and treatment.
- To predict patient diagnosis, aggregated data are used to speck early warning symptoms and mobilize resources to proactively address care.
- To increase interoperability and interconnectivity of healthcare (i.e., health information exchanges).
- To enhance patient care via mobile health, telemedicine, and self-tracking or home devices.

Storing and managing patient health information is a challenging task. Big data in medical field is crucial one. Ensuring patient data privacy and security is a significant challenge for any healthcare organization seeking to fulfill with the new rule. Any individual or organization that uses Protected Health Information (PHI) must comply, and this includes employees, physicians, vendors or other business associates, and other covered entities. Consider also that your compliance for data (small or big) must cover the following systems, processes, and policies:

- Registration systems
- Patient portals
- Patient financial systems
- Electronic medical records
- E-prescribing
- Business associate and vendor contracts
- Audits
- Notice of privacy practice

1.4.4 Visual Perception with Medical Data

Traditionally, healthcare has used business data far less regularly and comprehensively than most other industries. It has underinvested in advanced managerial technologies like reporting systems and data visualization. This may be partly due to some health-care providers viewing investments in managerial and operational information systems as less important than investments in clinical information systems. Whereas many organizations outside healthcare have developed or purchased real-time reporting systems that push targeted updates to specific end users, healthcare has typically relied on centralized production of static, undifferentiated report documents that provide the same view of historical performance to all recipients. Contemporary reporting systems often incorporate features such as interactive dashboards that provide customized, up-to-the-minute (or at least frequently updated) graphical displays of critical performance metrics, historical trends, and reference benchmarks or goals [25]. These dashboards are designed to help the end user focus on those data that are most informative about how their systems are performing. In healthcare, decision support dashboards are increasingly common on the clinical side, especially in EHR environments, but far less so when it comes to supporting managerial or operational decisions.

1.5 ANALYTICAL TECHNIQUES ON MEDICAL DATA

Healthcare data analytics includes the activities that include the collection of health-care data (patient behavior, clinical results, claims, and cost of incurring) to formulate a decision plan that involves discovery, interpretation, and exploring meaningful patterns in the data. Clinical data analytics plays a significant role in predicting the patient behavior, risk analysis, treatment cost reduction, and developing an analysis plan with the treatment concerned. The investigation of patterns across different types of healthcare data provides significance among the risks that tend to incur as a reflection toward treatment analysis. If risk analysis is foreseen in advance, the cost of treatment can be cut off to a great extent [26].

With the rapid development in tools and procedures over healthcare, it is necessary that healthcare data need to be analyzed for decision-making at proper intervals. Figure 1.2 provides an overview of healthcare data collection to knowledge discovery from data. The consistency of reports and documents with its requirements falls into the category of core medical data. Reducing the data variability and optimizing the risk factors provide medical experts to attain decision and interpretation at proper stages. The intervention in quality medicine is attained by delivering appropriate treatment with a stabilized patient care monitoring system. Thus, medical practitioners could attain the realm of disease-specific syndromes through the process and interventions made by predictive data models. The realm of healthcare data analytics aims at improvement in clinical practices by lowering risk factors.

1.5.1 Clinical Prediction Models

Clinical prediction models are most needed in the domain of healthcare technology. Different models have been used in practice for predicting different levels of syndromes [27]. At most, all the models deploy predictive mechanism with

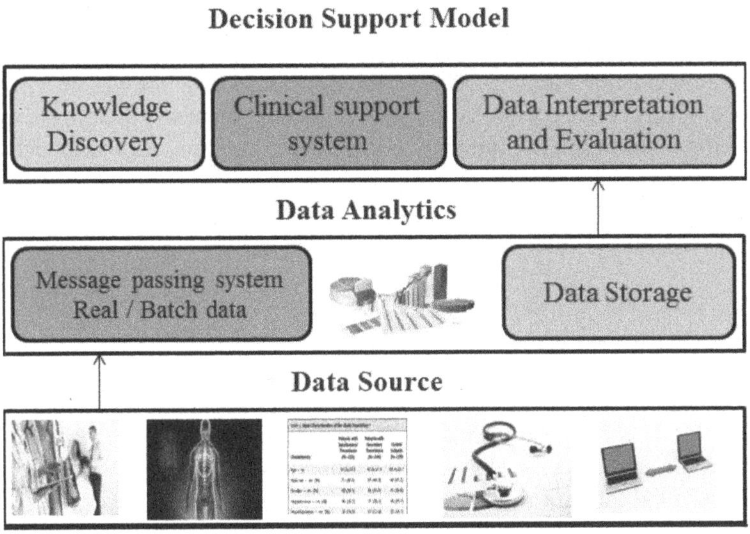

Decision Support Model

FIGURE 1.2   Healthcare analytics – an overview.

statistical significance. The outcome of the model provides the estimation of medical cost prediction, a region-based analysis of attribute determination, significance among the features, and the correlation patterns that exist among the attributes. Meanwhile, the type of the diagnostic problem with the risk of patient's behavior can also be analyzed with the prediction model.

1.5.1.1   Decision Trees

Over the years of the 1980s, Quinlan [28], a research scholar in the domain of machine learning, developed Iterative Dichotomiser 3 which is known to be the ID3, a decision tree algorithm. In accordance with this algorithm on ID3, the author proposed a successor of ID3 algorithm known to be the C4.5 algorithm. This algorithm became more familiar with data classification techniques corresponding to supervised learning systems. The algorithm ID3 is suitable for categorical decision criteria with smaller samples of data. The algorithm follows a greedy approach in the art of determining the local optimal value. Over-fitting of values may occur at stages where the algorithm fails to produce the optimal result on the given data.

Meanwhile, C4.5 has the ability to handle both continuous and categorical data with missing data, as well as attribute leveraging to different cost functions and tree pruning [29]. The next version to C4.5 is Quinlan-introduced C5.0 algorithm with memory competence and the capability to evaluate different sorts of attributes. On considering the working functionality of C4.5 algorithm, it is also called as the statistical algorithm upon data classification. It is also considered to be the good optimal algorithm for a better prediction and evaluation.

1.5.1.2   Artificial Neural Network

The functionality of Artificial Neural Network (ANN) is stimulated by biological neural systems in which nodes called 'neurons' have been combined together to formulate a weighted link to form network of neurons. The neuron is said to be the computing component which has adaptive weights which then produce the output based upon activation function. The perceptron neural function has only its input and output layers. The goal of this method is to solve problems in accordance with the working of human brain function. For the given attribute X_i, the model can be written as follows:

$$y_i = sign(X_i, W) \tag{1.1}$$

where the value of X_i is expressed as follows:

$$X_i = \left(x_{i0}, x_{i1}, x_{i2}, x_{i3} \cdots x_{ip}\right) \tag{1.2}$$

The value for X_i corresponds to the input vector (attribute) and W is the coefficient vector over the sign function. However, updating in weights over-fitting of the model is made using the rule function as follows:

$$w_j^{t+1} = w_j^t + \lambda\left(y_i - y_i^t\right)x_{ij} \tag{1.3}$$

In ANN, the estimation is made in accordance with the cost function, which then minimizes the mean squared error. This provides the squared difference between the observed and the estimated value. Because of this feature in determining the complexity in defining the minimum global value, gradient descent has been deployed, which then minimizes the cost function over the developed model. The effect of cost function won't be retrieved directly from the hidden nodes and also with the output information. Due to this phenomenon, backpropagation is being used for training the network of neurons. ANN is the ability to model complex function and strong mapping among the attributes. Hence, they are widely deployed in biomedical applications for making decisions upon varying medical criteria [30].

1.5.1.3 Kernel Methods

The principle behind kernel methods is that the attributes in the given search space are mapped to an abstract space, which provides the way to differentiate among multi-class classifications. The performance of kernel methods affords good results with data projection over large dimensions. The challenge behind kernel method lies in choosing the right kernel function for right data over evaluation [31]. Among the given data objects, the kernel function evaluates the similarity with the assignment in the highest value for kernel as $K(X, X')$. Various kernels such as polynomial, Gaussian, and sigmoid functions are widely used with varying parameters over experiments in medical data. In problems over heterogeneous data sources, kernel methods enhance the mechanism of data integration and formulation with an effect toward data analysis. The learning factor of the specified kernel will acquire its parameters in the feature space to deliver a robust estimation model. Multiple kernels with learning parameters have been widely used across biomedical applications where the model learns instantaneously in the given feature space [32].

1.5.1.4 Cost-Sensitive Methods

Clinical prediction models are typically developed with the aim to determine misclassification cost and test costs. Among all the types of various cost determination strategies, misclassification and test cost are the ones which eventually determine the efficacy of the computational algorithms. The model design in clinical prediction relies upon the computational cost and instability of the algorithms which need to be addressed with each sort of dataset. The data classification error is the one which is mainly influenced by misclassification cost function. In diagnosing a disease, the evaluation factors such as false-positive and false-positive error rates are the ones which need to be addressed in every analysis. When compared to false-positive results, false negative is the one which needs to be focused more seriously because it shows that the person has been moved to a dangerous state in diagnosis.

1.5.1.5 Naïve Bayes Classifier

The Naïve Bayes classification algorithm works according to the principle of the Bayes theorem, which is one among the standard strategies in mathematical statistics. It estimates the relationship between posterior probability and prior probability over a random event to occur. The theorem formulation is given as follows:

$$P(Y|X) = \frac{P(X|Y)P(Y)}{P(X)} \tag{1.4}$$

where $P(Y|X)$ is the possibility for the event Y which is conditioned over the event X. The Naïve Bayes classifier works according to the above formulation for an event to occur. The criterion in the classifier is comparing $P(Y = y \mid X_i)$ for diverse $y \in Y$ over the given set of X_i values such as $X_i = \{x_{i1}, x_{i2}, x_{i3} \cdots x_{in}\}$. In the Naïve Bayes classification algorithm, the values of X_i are supposed to be conditionally independent. Therefore, the values for $P(X_i \mid Y = y)$ are calculated using the following equation:

$$P(X_i \mid Y = y) = \prod_{k=1}^{P} P(x_{ik} \mid Y = y) \tag{1.5}$$

where the values for $P(x_{ik} \mid Y = y)$ can be estimated by k values using the training data. Hence, the conditional probability for the output value y is expressed as follows:

$$P(Y = y \mid X_i) \propto P(Y = y) \prod_{k=1}^{P} P(x_{ik} \mid Y = y) \tag{1.6}$$

As a result, the value for y that makes the most of above value is observed to be the exact output value [33]. More specifically, the Bayes classifier is adherently used up in prediction and in decision-making problems with attribute prediction on the highest accurate value.

REFERENCES

1. Weiss, Sholom M., Casimir A. Kulikowski, Saul Amarel, and Aran Safir. A Model-Based Method for Computer-Aided Medical Decision-Making. *Artificial Intelligence* 11, no. 1–2 (August 1978): 145–172. doi:10.1016/0004-3702(78)90015-2

2. Collen, M. F. The Origins of Informatics. *Journal of the American Medical Informatics Association* 1, no. 2 (March 1, 1994): 91–107. doi:10.1136/jamia.1994.95236152

3. Wong, Ka-Chun, ed. Computational Biology and Bioinformatics. (April 27, 2016). https://www.taylorfrancis.com/books/mono/10.1201/b20026/computational-biology-bioinformatics-ka-chun-wong

4. Radiological Society of North America Expert Consensus Statement on Reporting Chest CT Findings Related to COVID-19. Endorsed by the Society of Thoracic Radiology, the American College of Radiology, and RSNA. *Radiology: Cardiothoracic Imaging* 2, no. 2 (July 24, 2020): e200152. doi:10.1148/ryct.2020200152.podcast

5. B. Linden. Coronary Heart Disease - Prevention and Management. *Coronary Health Care* 3, no. 3 (1999): 159–163. doi:10.1016/S1362-3265(99)80010-8

6. Jesmin Nahar, Tasadduq Imam, Kevin S. Tickle, Yi-Ping Phoebe Chen. Computational Intelligence for Heart Disease Diagnosis: A Medical Knowledge Driven Approach. *Expert Systems with Applications* 40, no. 1 (2013): 96–104. doi:10.1016/j.eswa.2012.07.032

7. Population and the World Bank (Revised Edition). *Health, Nutrition, and Population* (January 2000). https://elibrary.worldbank.org/doi/abs/10.1596/0-8213-4663-6

8. Gupta, Indrani, and Pradeep Guin. Communicable Diseases in the South-East Asia Region of the World Health Organization: Towards a More Effective Response. *Bulletin of the World Health Organization* 88, no. 3 (March 1, 2010): 199–205. doi:10.2471/blt.09.065540

9. Yadav, Arvind Kumar, Kirtti Ranjan Paltasingh, and Pabitra Kumar Jena. Incidence of Communicable and Non-Communicable Diseases in India: Trends, Distributional Pattern and Determinants. *The Indian Economic Journal* 68, no. 4 (December 2020): 593–609. doi:10.1177/0019466221998841

10. Rosenbloom, S. Trent, Adrienne N. Crow, Jennifer Urbano Blackford, and Kevin B. Johnson. Cognitive Factors Influencing Perceptions of Clinical Documentation Tools. *Journal of Biomedical Informatics* 40, no. 2 (April 2007): 106–113. doi:10.1016/j.jbi.2006.06.006

11. T, Kulhanek. Infrastructure for Data Storage and Computation in Biomedical Research. *European Journal for Biomedical Informatics* 6, no. 01 (2010). doi:10.24105/ejbi.2010.06.1.10

12. Sarkar, I.N. Biomedical Informatics and Translational Medicine. *Journal of Translational Medicine* 8, no. 22 (2010). doi:10.1186/1479-5876-8-22

13. Special Issue on Community-driven Curation of Ontologies and Knowledge Bases in HealthCare and Life Sciences, *Journal of Biomedical Informatics* 44, no. 4 (2011): 507–508. doi:10.1016/j.jbi.2011.06.002

14. Indra Neil Sarkar. Biomedical Informatics and Translational Medicine. *Journal of Translational Medicine* 8, no. 1 (2010): 22–22. doi:10.1186/1479-5876-8-22

15. Sabyasachi Dash, Sushil Kumar, Shakyawar Mohit, Sharma Sandeep Kaushik. Big Data in Healthcare: Management, Analysis and Future Prospects. *Journal of Big Data* 6, no. 1 (2019): 1–25. doi:10.1186/S40537-019-0217-0

16. William M. Heroman, Charles B. Davis, Kenneth L. Farmer. Demand Forecasting and Capacity Management in Primary Care. *Physician Executive* 38, no. 1 (2012): 30–34

17. Alexander, M., Petersen, D., Rotolo, L., Leydesdorff. (2015). The Interaction of 'Supply', 'Demand', and 'Technological Capabilities' in Terms of Medical Subject Headings: A Triple Helix Model of Medical Innovation. arXiv: Digital Libraries.

18. Liwei Wang, Suraj Yerramilli, Akshay Iyer, Daniel W. Apley, Ping Zhu, Wei Chen. Scalable Gaussian Processes for Data-Driven Design Using Big Data with Categorical Factors. *Journal of Mechanical Design* 144, no. 2 (2022). doi:10.1115/1.4052221

19. Christos L. Stergiou, Konstantinos E. Psannis, Brij B. Gupta. InFeMo: Flexible Big Data Management through a Federated Cloud System. *ACM Transactions on Internet Technology* 22, no. 2 (2022): 1–22. doi:10.1145/3426972

20. Yosra Hajjaji, Wadii Boulila, Imed Riadh Farah, Imed Romdhani, Amir Hussain. Big Data and IoT-Based Applications in Smart Environments: A Systematic Review. *Computer Science Review* 39 (2021), 100318. doi:10.1016/J.COSREV.2020.100318

21. Jiabao Wen, Jiachen Yang, Bin Jiang, Houbing Song, Huihui Wang. Big Data Driven Marine Environment Information Forecasting: A Time Series Prediction Network. *IEEE Transactions on Fuzzy Systems* 29, no. 1 (2021): 4–18. doi:10.1109/TFUZZ.2020.3012393

22. Keke Gai, Meikang Qiu, Hui Zhao. Privacy-Preserving Data Encryption Strategy for Big Data in Mobile Cloud Computing. *IEEE Transactions on Big Data* 7, no. 4 (2021): 678–688. doi:10.1109/TBDATA.2017.2705807

23. Xiaokang Zhou, Yiyong Hu, Wei Liang, Jianhua Ma, Qun Jin. Variational LSTM Enhanced Anomaly Detection for Industrial Big Data. *IEEE Transactions on Industrial Informatics* 17, no. 5: 3469–3477. doi:10.1109/TII.2020.3022432

24. Christos Stergiou, Konstantinos E. Psannis, Brij B. Gupta. (2021). IoT-Based Big Data Secure Management in the Fog Over a 6G Wireless Network. *IEEE Internet of Things Journal* 8, no. 7 (2021): 5164–5171. doi:10.1109/JIOT.2020.3033131

25. Zhihan Lv, Ranran Lou, Jinhua Li, Amit Singh, Houbing Song. Big Data Analytics for 6G-Enabled Massive Internet of Things. *IEEE Internet of Things Journal* 8, no. 7 (2021): 5350–5359. doi:10.1109/JIOT.2021.3056128

26. Vinod C. Kaggal, Ravikumar Komandur Elayavilli, Saeed Mehrabi, Joshua J. Pankratz, Sunghwan Sohn, Yanshan Wang, Dingcheng Li, Majid Mojarad Rastegar, Sean P Murphy, Jason L. Ross, Rajeev Chaudhry, James D. Buntrock, Hongfang Liu. Toward a Learning Health-care System - Knowledge Delivery at the Point of Care Empowered by Big Data and NLP. *Biomed Inform Insights* 8, no. suppl 1 (2016): 13–22. doi:10.4137/BII.S37977

27. Alicia Curth, Patrick Thoral, Wilco van den Wildenberg, Peter Bijlstra, Daan P. de Bruin, Paul W. G. Elbers, Mattia Fornasa. Transferring Clinical Prediction Models Across Hospitals and Electronic Health Record Systems. Machine Learning and Knowledge Discovery in Databases: 605–621. https://researchinformation.amsterdamumc.org/en/publications/transferring-clinical-prediction-models-across-hospitals-and-elec-3

28. J., R., Quinlan. (1986). Induction of Decision Trees. *Machine Learning* 1, no. 1: 81–106. doi:10.1023/A:1022643204877

29. S.R. Safavian, David A. Landgrebe. A Survey of Decision Tree Classifier Methodology. *IEEE Transactions on Systems, Man, and Cybernetics* 21, no. 3 (1991): 660–674. doi:10.1109/21.97458

30. Frank Rosenblatt. The Perceptron: A Probabilistic Model for Information Storage and Organization in the Brain. *Psychological Review* 65, no. 6 (1958): 386–408. doi:10.1037/H0042519

31. Bernhard E. Boser, Isabelle Guyon, Vladimir Vapnik. A Training Algorithm for Optimal Margin Classifiers. (1992): 144–152. https://dl.acm.org/doi/10.1145/130385.130401

32. Shi Yu, Tillmann Falck, Anneleen Daemen, Léon-Charles Tranchevent, Johan A. K. Suykens, Bart De Moor, Yves Moreau. L2-Norm Multiple Kernel Learning and its Application to Biomedical Data Fusion. *BMC Bioinformatics* 11, no. 1 (2010): 309–309. doi:10.1186/1471-2105-11-309

33. Igor Kononenko. Inductive and Bayesian Learning in Medical Diagnosis. *Applied Artificial Intelligence* 7, no. 4 (1993): 317–337. doi:10.1080/08839519308949993

2 Statistical Methods and Swarm Intelligence Techniques in Clinical Data Prediction

2.1 SWARM INTELLIGENCE AN OVERVIEW

The term Swarm Intelligence was first coined by Gerardo Beni and Jing Wang toward the perspective of cellular robotic system [1]. Swarm intelligence corresponds to a collection of quantified algorithms that simulate natural learning behavior in a system of individuals that synchronize using self-organizing and distributed control mechanism. The working principle of the algorithms focuses toward the collective behavior inference, which results from interactions among individuals in the group and with the environment.

Algorithms such as Particle Swarm Optimization (PSO), Ant Colony Optimization (ACO), Bee-based Harmony Search (BHS), Stochastic Diffusion Search, Bat Algorithm, Multi-Swarm Optimization (MSO), and Cuckoo Search work according to the behavior of nature. A typical swarm intelligence system has some eminent properties such as:

- Group of individuals.
- Homogeneity among the group with respect to the environment.
- Learning ability and interaction among the group of individuals (local information) with respect to the environment.
- Global learning behavior as a result of the learning factor through local information with respect to the environment.

The research and application of swarm intelligence algorithms focus toward the collective behavior of birds resembling the character of flocking, pheromone set by the ants, schooling by fish, and microbiological intelligence.

2.2 SWARM INTELLIGENCE IN DATA PREDICTION AND DECISION-MAKING

Swarm Intelligence algorithms are widely used in a number of applications such as physical science, medical informatics, imaging, engineering, and data management services. The major consequence of Swarm Intelligence is to choose the best feasible solution, which results in the decision-making process. The process in swarm

DOI: 10.1201/9781003330189-2

intelligence has two major steps. First, problem formulation involves the assignment of decision variable, problem constraints, and objective function with a complete analysis over the problem domain. Second, it provides the solution to the observed problem by selecting appropriate mathematical function and test cases with an intention toward proper decision-making.

Feature selection in medical data paves the way for formulating a decision support system, which then serves as a tool for medical diagnosis, improving and monitoring patient care, and quality enhancements with improvements. The input data to the predictive model encompasses the training data consisting of all attributes for evaluation. Classification analysis alone may produce less interpretable and less accurate results. Feature selection along with data classification provides a data-driven decision support model with improved predictive power [2].

Mathematically, the perception in swarm intelligence can be defined as follows:

$$\text{Min}\_ f(x) \text{ or } \text{Max}\_ f(x) \text{ with } \left\{ x \in S \subset R^N \right\} \tag{2.1}$$

where $f(x)$ is the objective function that determines the efficacy of the model and x over the function is the N-dimensional space that consists of the feature attributes. The model to be developed over the vector space needs a solution search space over the point to generate local optimal and global optimal solution. The solution in the search space for $x^* \in S$ is a local optimal solution only if $\varepsilon < 0$ for $x \in S, f\left(x^*\right) \leq f(x)$. Correspondingly, the global maximum point for the values of x^* can be observed to be $x \in S \cap \left\{ x \mid \|x - x^*\| \leq \varepsilon \right\}$.

We can easily sort out the minimization problems in different forms of constraints with their assigned equivalent value. The art of swarm intelligence falls under metaheuristic approach with the intention of following an iterative approach. A near-optimal solution will be obtained with the process of assigning various learning strategies over the objective function [3]. The following are some of the widely used swarm intelligence techniques used for many sorts of real-time applications:

- Particle Swarm Optimization Algorithm
- Ant Colony Optimization Algorithm
- Bee Colony Algorithm
- Fish Swarm Algorithm
- Stochastic Diffusion Search Algorithm

Collective behavior of decentralized, self-organized systems is swarm intelligence, which can demonstrate intelligent behavior despite the absence of a centralized control mechanism [4]. The concept is inspired by the behavior of social species such as ants, bees, birds, and fish, which can accomplish complicated tasks by performing small individual acts. The study of algorithms and models inspired by natural systems constitutes swarm intelligence, a sort of artificial intelligence. Typically, these algorithms involve a large number of autonomous agents interacting with one another and their environment in order to achieve a specific goal. The agents may have limited capabilities and function according to simple rules, but via their interactions, they are able to develop emergent behavior that is more complicated and intelligent than any single agent could achieve on its own.

Ant colonies' behavior is an illustration of swarm intelligence. Individually, ants are basic organisms, yet collectively, they can organize themselves to find the shortest route from their nest to a food supply. Ants employ a mechanism known as stigmergy [5] to leave a trail of chemical that other ants can use to locate food. When more ants follow the trail, it strengthens and attracts other ants [5]. Ultimately, the entire colony is able to follow the route to the food source, despite the fact that no ant knows where the food is or the full path. The behavior of flocking birds is another instance of swarm intelligence. Without a centralized control mechanism, birds are able to fly in intricate formations, such as V-shaped patterns. Each bird in the flock adheres to a minimal set of norms, such as maintaining a minimum distance from other birds and following the flock's direction. With these simple interactions, the flock can demonstrate coordinated behavior that enables it to traverse the environment and fly more efficiently.

There are numerous applications for swarm intelligence, including optimization, robotics, and sensor networks. The employment of swarm intelligence algorithms to optimize supply chain management is one example. In this instance, the agents represent various components of the supply chain, and the objective is to optimize the flow of commodities and data between them. The swarm intelligence algorithm can aid in identifying supply chain bottlenecks and inefficiencies and recommend strategies to improve them.

2.2.1 CHARACTERISTICS OF SWARM INTELLIGENCE

1. Robustness and adaptability

Robustness and adaptability are two essential features of swarm intelligence algorithms. These qualities allow the algorithms to effectively handle uncertainty and environmental changes, making them applicable to a wide variety of applications [6].

Robustness is the capacity of a system to retain its functionality regardless of external shocks or environmental changes. In the context of swarm intelligence, robustness refers to the ability of the algorithm to continue doing its task even if there are disturbances or changes in the environment or if some agents in the swarm fail to function as planned. This is because swarm intelligence algorithms are designed to function in a decentralized and self-organized fashion, with each agent acting independently based on simple principles. Hence, even if one or more agents fail, the remainder of the swarm can continue to function and accomplish the desired result [7]. Consider a swarm of robots charged with exploring an unknown environment as an example. If one or more robots malfunction or are damaged, the remainder of the swarm is unaffected and can continue investigating the area. The remaining robots are able to modify their behavior to compensate for the lost robots and continue to efficiently investigate the area.

Adaptability is the capacity of a system to modify its behavior in response to environmental changes. In the context of swarm intelligence, adaptability refers to the algorithm's ability to modify its behavior and decision-making process in response to environmental or task-specific changes. Rather than depending on a centralized decision-making process, swarm intelligence algorithms are designed to work on the basis of local knowledge and basic principles. Consider, for instance, a swarm of drones assigned to monitor a forest for wildfires. As environmental variables such as wind direction or humidity change, the swarm can adapt its behavior by modifying the drones' flight patterns and the locations they are monitoring. The ability of the drones to communicate and adapt their behavior depending on fresh knowledge enables the swarm to effectively respond to environmental changes.

2. Scalability

A fundamental advantage of swarm intelligence algorithms is their scalability. Scalability refers to an algorithm's capacity to manage a growing number of agents and tasks while preserving its performance and efficiency. Due to their operation based on basic rules and decentralized decision-making, swarm intelligence algorithms are inherently scalable. Each agent in the swarm adheres to a set of rules based on local information, allowing the swarm to operate efficiently despite its huge size [4]. In addition, the decentralized decision-making process enables the swarm to do complicated tasks that would be challenging to manage with a centralized control system. Consider, for instance, a swarm of robots entrusted with optimizing the flow of commodities throughout a complex supply chain. The swarm can consist of hundreds or even thousands of robots, each of which is responsible for a specific supply chain operation, such as shipping or packaging. Each robot can make decisions based on local knowledge, and the swarm can operate based on simple criteria such as decreasing the time between each supply chain stage. This enables the swarm to effectively manage a vast number of tasks and agents without requiring a centralized decision-making procedure [8].

Swarm intelligence algorithms are also scalable in terms of computational complexity. Several swarm intelligence algorithms have a low computing cost, allowing them to address large-scale issues more efficiently than other optimization techniques, such as genetic algorithms and simulated annealing. This makes swarm intelligence algorithms applicable in contexts with limited resources, such as sensor networks [4]. Consider, for instance, a sensor network tasked with monitoring a vast area for temperature or humidity changes. The sensor network may include hundreds or even thousands of sensors, each of which is responsible for monitoring a distinct area. Using a swarm intelligence algorithm, the location of sensors can be optimized to reduce the number of sensors required while retaining an accurate measurement of the environment. The algorithm can function based on simple rules, such as maximizing the sensor network's coverage while minimizing sensor overlap. This allows the method to efficiently manage a large number of sensors without incurring a huge computational cost. The decentralized decision-making process and low computational cost allow swarm intelligence algorithms to operate efficiently and effectively in a variety of applications, from supply chain optimization to sensor network management.

3. Creativity

One of the benefits of swarm intelligence is its capacity to produce new and original problem solutions. Algorithms based on swarm intelligence can generate solutions that exceed the capability of individual agents and conventional optimization techniques. This is due to the fact that swarm intelligence algorithms function on the basis of simple rules and decentralized decision-making, allowing the formation of unique and unexpected solutions. The creativity advantage of swarm intelligence is especially effective in problem-solving situations requiring a high degree of creativity or originality, such as product design, art, and music. In such situations, the diversity of the swarm and the agents' capacity to explore a wide variety of solutions might result in unusual and unexpected outcomes.

Consider, for instance, a swarm of robots tasked with the creation of a new product. The robots can operate according to a simple set of principles, such as maximizing the product's utility while decreasing its cost. Each robot is able to suggest a design based on its local knowledge and share it with the other robots [4]. The swarm can then converge on a solution that is both original and functional, with each robot adding its own perspective and expertise. In the realms of art and music, swarm intelligence also provides a creative advantage. By using the diversity and exploration capabilities of the swarm, algorithms utilizing swarm intelligence can be employed to make original artwork or music. In these cases, agents can function based on simple parameters, such as maximizing the diversity of the artwork or musical notes, and can explore a vast array of options to generate surprising and innovative results. Swarm intelligence can also be utilized to address challenges requiring a high level of creativity, such as those encountered in scientific research. Algorithms employing swarm intelligence can be used to optimize experiments, simulations, and data analysis by examining a broad variety of alternatives and suggesting unique solutions. The diversity of the swarm and the agents' capacity to seek alternative solutions can result in novel and surprising findings.

4. Low computational cost

The low computing cost of swarm intelligence algorithms is one of their advantages. This indicates that swarm intelligence algorithms are able to handle difficult optimization problems with relatively modest computational resources. This benefit makes swarm intelligence algorithms a desirable option for real-world situations requiring quick and effective answers. Typically, swarm intelligence systems rely on simple rules and decentralized decision-making. Each agent in the swarm adheres to a set of rules that enables it to interact with other agents and the environment without the need for a centralized control mechanism [4]. This strategy decreases the algorithm's computational complexity because each agent just needs to examine its local information when making decisions. Additionally, the decentralized decision-making mechanism enables the swarm to operate in a distributed fashion, hence reducing the computing cost. The low computational cost benefit of swarm intelligence algorithms is particularly advantageous in applications with limited computing resources, such as embedded systems, mobile devices, and sensor networks, where computer resources are constrained. In these applications, algorithms employing swarm intelligence can optimize resource allocation, scheduling, and energy consumption while minimizing computational expense.

Consider, for instance, a swarm of drones tasked with maximizing package delivery. The drones can function in accordance with a set of simple criteria, such as limiting travel distance and delivery time while avoiding collisions with other drones and objects. Without a centralized control system, the swarm may then optimize the distribution of items to drones based on their position and availability. This strategy can lower the computing cost of the optimization procedure, enabling the swarm to operate effectively and efficiently in real-world circumstances: In the field of sensor networks, swarm intelligence demonstrates its cheap computing cost advantage once again. Sensor networks are comprised of numerous sensors that collect environmental data and transfer it to a central server for analysis. Algorithms employing swarm intelligence can optimize the placement of sensors to improve network coverage while minimizing energy consumption. The agents in the swarm can do this optimization using basic principles, such as maximizing the distance between sensors and limiting the overlap between their coverage regions. This method can lower the computing cost of the optimization procedure, enabling the sensor network to operate effectively and efficiently.

5. Real-world applicability

Swarm intelligence algorithms have numerous real-world applications across a wide range of domains, including robotics, transportation, logistics, manufacturing, and agriculture. The advantages of swarm intelligence, such as adaptability, scalability, robustness, low computational cost, and creativity, make it a powerful tool for solving complex optimization problems in real-world scenarios.

2.2.2 SWARM INTELLIGENCE TECHNIQUES

2.2.2.1 Particle Swarm Optimization Algorithm

Particle swarm optimization (PSO) is a meta-heuristic optimization technique modeled after the social behavior of animals like birds and fish. The technique employs a population of particles that traverse the search space in order to identify the optimal solution to a given problem. Each particle indicates a feasible resolution to the issue and advances through the search space based on its current position and velocity, as well as the optimal position discovered by the particle itself and by the swarm as a whole. The PSO method begins by seeding a random population of particles across the search space. Each particle is given a place and initial velocity. The position of the particle represents a potential solution to the optimization problem, while its velocity shows the direction and speed with which it traverses the search space.

For each algorithm iteration, each particle's position and velocity are modified according to the following equations:

$$\text{velocity}(i+1) = w * \text{velocity}(i) + c1 * \text{rand}() *$$

$$\left(\text{best\_position\_particle} - \text{position\_particle}\right) +$$

$$c2 * \text{rand}() * \left(\text{best\_position\_swarm} - \text{position\_particle}\right)$$
$$\text{position}(i+1) = \text{position}(i) + \text{velocity}(i+1)$$

where 'i' is the current iteration, w is the inertia mass, $c1$ and $c2$ represent coefficient of acceleration, rand() denotes a random number between 0 and 1, best_position_ particle is the best position found by the particle, and best_position_swarm is the best position found by the swarm as a whole. The velocity equation modifies the particle's velocity based on its present velocity, the distance to its optimal position, and the distance to the optimal position of the swarm. The position equation adjusts the particle's position based on the particle's current position and velocity.

The method iterates until a stopping requirement, such as a maximum number of iterations or a minimal error tolerance, is fulfilled. The optimal solution to the problem is the best place determined by the swarm. PSO has various benefits over alternative optimization techniques. It is simple to build and requires no gradient information, making it appropriate for non-linear and non-convex situations. Additionally, it is good at locating global optimums and can manage many optimums. PSO has been applied to numerous challenges, including neural network optimization, image processing, financial forecasting, and robotics. PSO has been utilized, for instance, to maximize the performance of unmanned aerial vehicles (UAVs) during surveillance missions [9]. The algorithm optimizes the UAVs' flight route depending on their positions and velocities, as well as the positions of the targets to be monitored. PSO has also been used to optimize the allocation of resources in a supply chain network, hence increasing the supply chain's efficiency and decreasing its costs.

In conclusion, PSO is an effective optimization algorithm that employs a population of particles to seek the optimal solution to a given issue. The technique is efficient in locating global optimums, simple to construct, and capable of dealing with non-linear and non-convex issues. PSO has several applications in the real world, including UAV surveillance and supply chain efficiency.

2.2.2.2 Ant Colony Optimization Algorithm

Ant colony optimization (ACO) is a meta-heuristic approach for optimizing based on ant colony data. The algorithm imitates the manner in which ants forage for food by creating pheromone trails that other ants follow to locate the food source. ACO has been used for numerous optimization problems, including the Traveling Salesman Problem (TSP), the Vehicle Routing Problem (VRP), and the Job Shop Scheduling Problem (JSSP).

The ACO algorithm operates by imitating an ant colony's behavior as it searches for food. The algorithm initiates a population of virtual ants at the first point of the optimization issue. Each ant is given a current position and is permitted to travel through the search space according to a set of rules designed to simulate the behavior of real ants [5]. When ants traverse the search area, they leave behind pheromone trails that entice other ants to follow the same path. Because pheromone trails dissipate over time, the trails that lead to superior solutions are reinforced by more frequent pheromone deposits, whereas the trails that lead to inferior solutions evaporate more rapidly. The ACO algorithm repeats several cycles of ant movement, pheromone deposition, and evaporation until a stopping requirement, such as a maximum number of iterations or a minimal error tolerance, is met. The problem's optimal solution is returned as the best solution found by the colony.

The ACO algorithm employs a set of rules to determine how each ant determines its next action. These provisions include:

- Areas with high pheromone concentrations attract ants. This resembles the behavior of actual ants, which follow pheromone trails to locate food.
- Moreover, regions with a shorter journey to their objective are attractive to ants. This motivates the ants to march toward the objective.
- Ants update the pheromone trails based on the quality of the solutions they find. This motivates ants to follow pheromone trails that lead to superior solutions.

ACO has a number of benefits over alternative optimization techniques. Even in complex, high-dimensional search spaces, it is remarkably effective at locating global optimums. It can accommodate many objectives and constraints, making it suited for a vast array of optimization issues. Therefore, ACO is quite simple to build and requires no gradient information. ACO has been applied to a variety of challenges, including transportation routing issues, network optimization, and scheduling issues [5]. ACO has been used, for instance, to improve the routes of delivery trucks, thereby reducing transportation costs and enhancing delivery times. Moreover, the technique has been utilized to optimize the design of computer networks, hence enhancing network efficiency and minimizing expenses. ACO is a powerful optimization technique that mimics the behavior of real ants to discover the optimal solution to a given problem. The method is efficient in locating global optimums, simple to implement, and capable of accommodating numerous objectives and restrictions. ACO has several applications in the real world, including transportation routing and network optimization.

2.2.2.3   Bee Colony Algorithm

BHS is a meta-heuristic optimization technique inspired by honeybee behavior during nectar foraging. In 2011, Yang et al. introduced the algorithm as an extension of the Harmony Search (HS) technique [10]. The BHS algorithm operates by imitating the foraging behavior of a honeybee colony. The algorithm initiates a population of virtual bees at the first point of the optimization issue. Each bee is assigned a current position and allowed to roam the search space according to a set of rules designed to replicate the behavior of real bees.

By executing a waggle dance, bees communicate the location and quality of food sources as they move across the search space. This communication is mirrored in BHS by a set of rules designed to find a balance between exploration and exploitation [9]. The BHS method repeats many cycles of bee movement, communication, and update until a stopping requirement, such as a maximum number of iterations or a minimal error tolerance, is fulfilled. The problem's optimal solution is returned as the best solution found by the colony.

The BHS algorithm employs a set of criteria to determine how bees choose their next action. These provisions include:

- Bees are drawn to regions with abundant, nutritious food sources. This imitates the behavior of real bees, which use the waggle dance to locate food.
- Moreover, regions with a shorter distance to food sources attract bees. This motivates the bees to proceed toward the objective.
- The quality of the food source is modified in accordance with the quality of the bees' solutions. This stimulates the bees to explore new places and make use of the greatest locations.

BHS has a number of benefits over alternative optimization algorithms. Even in complex, high-dimensional search spaces, it is remarkably effective at locating global optimums. It can accommodate many objectives and constraints, making it suitable for a vast array of optimization issues. Furthermore, BHS is quite simple to construct and requires no gradient information.

BHS has been applied to numerous challenges, including engineering design, data mining, and image processing. BHS has been utilized, for instance, to optimize the design of heat exchangers, thereby lowering energy consumption and increasing efficiency. Moreover, the method has been utilized to optimize data mining algorithms, hence enhancing the precision and efficacy of data analysis. BHS is a potent optimization method that imitates honeybee behavior to find the ideal solution to a given problem. The method is efficient in locating global optimums, simple to implement, and capable of accommodating numerous objectives and restrictions. BHS has several applications in the real world, including engineering design and data mining.

2.2.2.4 Fish Swarm Algorithm

Artificial fish swarm intelligence (AFSI) is a technique of artificial intelligence based on the behavior of real fish in groups [11]. It incorporates a set of artificial creatures known as artificial fish that interact with their surroundings and with one another to solve optimization problems. AFSI was inspired by the behavior of fish, which are known for their ability to coordinate and collaborate in groups in order to obtain food, escape predators, and move to new regions. The behavior of fish is guided by a series of simple rules, such as following the path of other fish, migrating toward food-rich areas, and avoiding obstacles [11]. Each artificial fish in AFSI is represented by a point in a multidimensional search space, and the objective is to identify the optimal solution to a given optimization problem [7]. The artificial fish swim around the search space, searching for the optimal solution based on a set of behavioral guidelines.

Using three primary components, the behavior of artificial fish is modeled:

- Each artificial fish navigates the search space with a random walk strategy. The movement direction and velocity are determined by the position of other fish and the value of the objective function.
- Feeding: Each fake fish determines the quality of the solution based on its present position and the positions of other fish in its proximity. On the basis of this judgment, the fish modifies its movement in an effort to reach better solutions.
- Artificial fish tend to congregate in regions with high concentrations of high-quality solutions. This behavior enables the fish to explore the search space more efficiently and arrive at superior answers.

The AFSI algorithm functions by initializing a school of artificial fish in the search space and changing their placements iteratively based on their behavior. The method continues until a termination requirement, such as a maximum number of iterations or a degree of convergence, is fulfilled. AFSI has been used for numerous optimization challenges, such as engineering design, data mining, image processing, and pattern recognition. It has been demonstrated to be effective at locating high-quality solutions at a relatively cheap computational cost when compared to other optimization strategies [12]. In conclusion, artificial fish swarm intelligence is a technique of computational intelligence based on the behavior of real fish in groups. It involves a set of artificial agents that interact with their surroundings and with one another in order to solve optimization challenges. The method models the behavior of artificial fish by utilizing movement, feeding, and grouping components and updates the fish's positions iteratively until a termination criterion is fulfilled.

In order to optimize the performance of swarm intelligence algorithms, there are a number of parameters that can be adjusted. These parameters can be classified into two major categories: algorithm-specific parameters and problem-specific parameters.

Algorithm-specific parameters are the parameters that are unique to a certain swarm intelligence algorithm. In PSO, for instance, the algorithm-specific parameters are the number of particles, their maximum velocity, and their inertia weight [13]. The algorithm-specific parameters for ACO consist of the pheromone evaporation rate, the exploration factor, and the exploitation factor. The algorithm-specific parameters of BCO consist of the number of scout bees, the number of worker bees, and the number of observer bees.

In contrast, problem-specific parameters are parameters that are unique to the optimization problem being solved. For instance, the problem-specific parameters in a function optimization problem include the number of variables, the search space, and the fitness function. To evaluate the effectiveness of swarm intelligence algorithms, it is required to tailor their parameters to the given task. There is no single set of parameters applicable to all problems [7]. Thus, it is necessary to experiment with various parameter values to determine the optimal combination for a given problem. In general, algorithm-specific parameters with greater values, such as the number of particles or bees, tend to enhance the algorithm's exploration capability, whereas smaller values tend to promote exploitation. Similarly, larger problem-specific characteristics, such as the size of the search area, necessitate a greater capacity for exploration, whereas simpler issues with smaller search spaces may necessitate a greater capacity for exploitation.

2.3 STATISTICAL APPROACHES IN MEDICAL DATA ANALYTICS

Statistical learning denotes the applicability of statistical tools for effective modeling, data analysis, and understanding the patterns over complex datasets. Statistical data analysis with intersections in the field of healthcare informatics and machine learning have become exploiting with a high demand across disciplines. In the beginning of nineteenth century, Gauss and Legendre proposed research articles in the concept of 'method of least squares', which is the earlier version now termed as linear regression analysis [14].

Regression analysis has been used widely over quantitative data for prediction across applications. To analyze qualitative data, Fisher proposed 'Linear Discriminant Analysis' (LDA) for effective prediction which has been extensively used in clinical field and stock data analysis [15]. Over the years, various authors proposed different techniques for statistical evaluation such as regression analysis, generalized models, and its variants. Generalized models encompass the incorporation of linear regression and logistic regression for computational evaluation [16].

By the 1980s, the field of technology had improved significantly with the statistical approaches experimented over time. The implementation of non-linear methods was found to be no longer cost sensitive. Data classification and regression trees were proposed by [17] with the interpretation of cross validation in model selection. Generalized additive models play a vital role in statistical data analysis, with an extension toward linear data models for effective prediction over medical data. In medical data analysis, statistical tools have been intended for the analysis of observed evidences that contribute to the cause, occurrence of disease, and the risk factors that subsidize to the disease.

Locating metabolic syndromes and their risk factors provides an efficient way for clinical interventions and investigations. The development of predictive models using statistical techniques makes medical practitioners have a better clinical analysis and research interferences. Regression analysis such as logistic regression and cox regression has been used to evaluate that metabolomics that offer significant contribution toward type II diabetes [18]. The inference shows that 16 and 17 metabolites have been selected for logistic and cox regression with AROC values of about 90% and 73% respectively. Hence, regression analysis over medical data improves the prediction in type II diabetes and its risk factors with clinical rationality and interventions. Similar suggestions can be incorporated in medical diagnosis to have an analysis of medical data.

In predictive analytics, the goal is to develop a data analytic model that predicts the objective measure of importance. The objective measure is then used up to simulate the process of learning scheme. The mechanism of data prediction can be formulated as classification and regression models. The target variable during classification and regression process plays a significant role in model development.

2.3.1 REGRESSION ANALYSIS

Regression analysis is a measure of determining the relationship between two or more variables with respect to the unit measurements. In practice, there are various types of regressions with which applicability over the determination of relation that signifies between two or more than two variables can be decided. The variable whose value is about to be predicted is said to be the reliant on variable and the variable that influences the prediction is said to be the independent variable. In a bivariate distribution, the curve of regression with the curve representing the straight line is said to be straight line linear regression. If the curve of regression does not represent a straight line, then it is of type curvilinear.

In a bivariate distribution $(x_i, y_i); i = 1, 2, 3, \cdots, n$; let Y represent the dependent variable and X the independent variable. Then, the line of regression is given by the following equation as Y on X to be:

$$Y = mX + c \qquad (2.2)$$

The major consequence is to determine the coefficients m and c by finding the 'best fit' by the principle of least squares with the intention of minimizing the sum of the squares of deviation. According to the principle of least squares, the values of m and c are determined by the following equation:

$$E = \sum_{i=1}^{n} P_i H_i^2 = \sum_{i=1}^{n} (y_i - c - mx_i)^2 \qquad (2.3)$$

The values of m and c should be found to be minimum in accordance with the line of best fit. In the realm of practical statistics, the relation between the observed variables can be expressed in terms of algebraic expression such as logarithmic, exponential, and polynomial functions. More specifically, it can be used to determine the value of one variable with correspondence to another representing its values.

2.3.2 LINEAR DISCRIMINANT ANALYSIS

The objective behind the Linear Discriminant Analysis (LDA) is to determine the linear arrangement of feature that illustrates the mechanism among two or more classes. The resulting feature set can be used for classifier evaluation, which then is said to be a dimensionality reduction. The independent variable in the given space is ordinarily distributed which is one of the assumptions in LDA data models. More specifically, LDA can be estimated for two class dataset, multiclass dataset, and incremental dataset. The maximization among the class separable variables can be observed along the axis of separation in the given plane.

In a given population, P_i is the density function for x in a given plane with mean μ_i, and then the LDA function of x with respect to the population is given by the following equation:

$$f(x \mid P_i) = \frac{1}{(2\Pi)^{p/2} |\Sigma|^{1/2}} \exp\left[-\frac{1}{2}(x - \mu_i)' \Sigma^{-1}(x - \mu_i)\right] \qquad (2.4)$$

LDA has its consequence when the variance–covariance matrix won't have any dependency upon the entire population P_i from which the values are observed. For this criterion, the decision is based upon the score function value for the given population P_i. The score function is expressed as follows:

$$S(X) = d_{i0} + \sum_{j=1}^{p} d_{ij} x_j + \log p_i \qquad (2.5)$$

The above expression exhibits a regression model intercept d_{i0} and constant d_{ij}. The LDA model has its variants in Quadratic Discriminant Analysis and Regularized Discriminant Analysis [19]. If there are more than two segregations in class label assumptions, LDA can be applied with more parametric assumptions in developing the predictive model [20].

2.3.3 Correlation Analysis

In a bivariate data distribution, the interesting measure is to spot out if there is any correlation among the targeted two variables. For the given two variables, if the modification in one of the variable upsets the modification in the other variable, then the variables are found to be correlated to one another. Correlation among the bivariate data is of positive correlation and negative correlation.

If the increase or decrease in one variable shows a significant increase or decrease in another variable, then the correlation is said to be of positive correlation when the deviation is in same direction of intent. However, if the deviation of intent is in opposite direction, the correlation is said to be of type negative. Correlation among the variable is perfect when the deviation in one variable is proportional to that of the deviation in another.

2.3.3.1 Karl Pearson's Coefficient of Correlation

The measure of degree of linear relationship between two variables can be computed using Karl Pearson correlation coefficient [21]. For the given two arbitrary variables X and Y, the correlations are given by $r(X,Y)$ in which the linear relationship is given as follows:

$$r(X,Y) = \frac{\text{Cov}(X,Y)}{\sigma_X \sigma_Y} \qquad (2.6)$$

In the given function (x_i, y_i) for $i = 1, 2, 3, \cdots, n$ distribution, the relationship is given as follows:

$$\text{Cov}(X,Y) = E\left[(X - E(X))(Y - E(Y))\right] \qquad (2.7)$$

It should be observed that $r(X,Y)$ provides a linear combination of relation between the variables X and Y. The limit function for the correlation is given as follows:

$$r(X,Y) = \frac{\text{Cov}(X,Y)}{\sigma_X \sigma_Y} = \frac{\dfrac{1}{n}\sum (x_i - \bar{x})(y_i - \bar{y})}{\left[\dfrac{1}{n}\sum (x_i - \bar{x})^2 \bullet \dfrac{1}{n}(y_i - \bar{y})^2\right]^{1/2}} \qquad (2.8)$$

$$r^2(X,Y) = \frac{\left(\displaystyle\sum_i a_i b_i\right)^2}{\left(\displaystyle\sum_i a_i^2\right)\left(\displaystyle\sum_i b_i^2\right)} \qquad (2.9)$$

From equation (2.9) using the Schwartz inequality, the limit value is expressed as follows:

$$r^2(X,Y) \le 1 \,|\, r(X,Y) | \le 1 \Rightarrow -1 \le r(X,Y) \le 1 \qquad (2.10)$$

As a result, the value of correlation coefficient won't exceed the unity value numerically. It lies between the range of -1 and $+1$. For the values of $r = +1$, the correlation coefficient is said to be perfect and found to be positive, and for $r = -1$, the correlation is perfect and negative in value.

2.3.3.2 Spearman's Rank Correlation Coefficient

Let $(x_i, y_i); i = 1, 2, 3, \cdots, n$ be the given ranks of the ith individual in a given group of records by considering two characteristics, say A and B, and then the Pearsonian coefficient of association among the ranks' $x_i's$ and $y_i's$ is the rank correlation coefficient between the characteristics A and B over the defined set of individuals [22]. If the variable takes the values $1, 2, 3, \ldots, n$, then the formulation is expressed as follows:

$$\bar{x} = \bar{y} = \frac{1}{n}(1 + 2 + 3 + \cdots + n) = \frac{n+1}{2} \qquad (2.11)$$

$$\sigma_{x^2} = \frac{1}{n}\sum_{i=1}^{n} x_i^2 - \bar{x}^2 = \frac{1}{n}(1^2 + 2^2 + 3^2 + \cdots + n^2) - \left(\frac{n+1}{2}\right)^2 \qquad$$

$$= \frac{n(n+1)(2n+1)}{6n} - \left(\frac{n+1}{2}\right)^2 = \frac{n^2-1}{12} \qquad (2.12)$$

Upon computation, equation (2.12) is expressed as follows:

$$\rho = 1 - \frac{\sum\limits_{i=1}^{n} d_i^2}{2n\sigma_{x^2}} = 1 - \frac{6\sum\limits_{i=1}^{n} d_i^2}{n(n^2-1)} \tag{2.13}$$

The above formulation is Spearman's rank correlation between the defined set of individuals. The correctness in calculation of correlation among the set of individuals with its characteristics can be evaluated using the following equation:

$$\sum d_i = \sum (x_i - y_i) = \sum x_i - \sum y_i = n(\bar{x} - \bar{y}) = 0 \tag{2.14}$$

2.3.3.3 Chi-Squared Analysis

Chi-square variate is the square of standard normal variate with 1 degree of freedom as for $X_i\,(i = 1, 2, 3, \ldots, n)$ with n representing self-regulating normal variates representing the mean value μ_i and variance $\sigma_i^2\,(i = 1, 2, 3, \ldots, n)$, then Chi-square is given by the following equation:

$$\chi^2 = \sum_{i=1}^{n} \left(\frac{X_i - \mu_i}{\sigma_i} \right)^2 \tag{2.15}$$

If $X \sim \chi^2_{(n)}$, then the characteristic function of χ^2 distribution is expressed as follows:

$$\phi_X(t) = E\{\exp(itX)\} = \int_0^\infty \exp(itx) f(x)\, dx \tag{2.16}$$

$$\phi_X(t) = \frac{1}{2^{n/2}\Gamma(n/2)} \int_0^\infty \exp\left\{-\left(\frac{1-2it}{x}\right)x\right\}(x)^{\frac{n}{2}-1}\, dx = (1 - 2it)^{-n/2} \tag{2.17}$$

The measure of Chi-square analysis helps to determine the degree of discrepancy between the observed and expected frequencies in a given distribution as in equation (2.17). The value of Chi-square is defined to be the non-parametric test. Hence, the value is not derived from the given set of observations in a population. A testing of hypothesis is made to determine whether the accepted or rejected condition is met as a conclusion with the given statistical population.

2.4 DIAGNOSTIC EVALUATION BY RECEIVER OPERATING CHARACTERISTIC CURVE

In statistics and analytics, the Receiver Operating Characteristic (ROC) curve is plotted True Positives against False Positives upon several threshold parametric settings. The diagnostic intervention of the disease stipulation and its discrimination

TABLE 2.1

Separation among Test Cases with Disease Status

Test Results	Disease Statistics				
	Present	Cases	Absent	Cases	Total
Positive cases	True Positive (TP)	p	False Positive (FP)	x	$p + x$
Negative cases	False Negative (FN)	q	True Negative (TN)	y	$q + y$
Total		$p + q$		$x + y$	$N = p + q + x + y$

can be learned from ROC curve analysis. The distribution of data with probabilistic estimate across both the directions can be observed significantly with discrimination in the threshold value.

The performance in a diagnostic evaluation can be plotted with normal against abnormal data records, which can be observed over the plot [23]. The leverage in variation between sensitivity and the false positive rate provides the exact disease separation among the classes. As an outcome, the cases can be significantly addressed in Table 2.1.

During the diagnostic test determination using ROC, the confidence level has to be set with optimal criterion value. If the disease prevalence is known, then the cost of decision upon FP, FN, TP, and TN can be determined with parametric estimation. The neutral condition in cost estimation can be addressed only if $\left(FP_c - TN_c \right) / \left(FN_c - TP_c \right) = 1$ upon estimation.

2.5 SUMMARY OF SWARM INTELLIGENCE IN BIOMEDICAL INFORMATICS

The role of swarm intelligence algorithms and data classification in biomedical engineering is an emerging domain for research in building a real-world decision support system. Determining healthcare issues and resolving its inconsistencies are big problems. In the domain of healthcare analytics, the mechanism to identify valid, useful, and ultimately understandable with relevant data patterns has to be determined over the dataset. The algorithm in data classification helps in the detection and analysis of high-dimensional healthcare records with disease detection and investigation.

Data classification and prediction fall over the interface between statistical reporting with the intent of discovering new insights which can be operationalized. Healthcare data can be viewed as a thought of:

- Real-time healthcare analysis
- Batch-based healthcare analysis

In the data analysis of real-time systems, active measures will be taken with the analysis of a set of patients' records with the aim of providing prescriptive decisions. Each of the patients will be treated with care and concern during each step of the analysis process. Meanwhile, the process of batch-based healthcare data analysis evaluates and decides upon the dataset that corresponds to a specific group of population. Therefore, batch-based analysis decides upon the decision for a particular kind of disease over a large medical system, which then provides the effectiveness in enhancing the disease management system. This decision support system paves the pathway for medical data assessment for population-based healthcare information system.

Medical data analysis emphasizes the utilization of computer knowledge in fields such as therapeutic research, assistive healthcare, and instinctual medical learning. It resolves the problems and risk-related impacts in health technology in order to provide a valued health information service. Computer-aided diagnosis and service provides automated decision support data analysis for the recommendation of model-based actions for the risk factors associated with the specific disease.

Technological innovations in medical sciences mainly target the development of algorithmic models and tools with specific measures mainly to disseminate the risk and to control disease-specific syndromes. In order to explore the medical issues and its originating factors, the risk related to the disease has to be clearly identified. From the medical point of view corresponding to cardiac disease and its risk factors, several research institutes desire the incorporation and the development of advanced technological solutions corresponding to the disease. The implication of disease-specific risk factors varies from region to region with diverse significance. Identifying such a disease-specific risk and its implications across a specific region is a major task to computer-aided diagnosis in medical informatics. Determination of disease-specific risk factor with the aim of solving its inconsistencies by developing a decision support model over region-based analysis is the key motto behind this research work. A better understanding and most effective interventions are needed for reducing the risk with respect to the location, likelihood, and dietary habits concerned with each group of people.

REFERENCES

1. Gerardo Beni, Jing Wang. (1993). Swarm Intelligence in Cellular Robotic Systems, 703–712. https://link.springer.com/chapter/10.1007/978-3-642-58069-7_38
2. Shamsul Huda, John Yearwood, Herbert F. Jelinek, Mohammad Mehedi Hassan, Giancarlo Fortino, Michael E. Buckland. (2016). A Hybrid Feature Selection with Ensemble Classification for Imbalanced Healthcare Data: A Case Study for Brain Tumor Diagnosis. *IEEE Access*, 4, 9145–9154. doi:10.1109/ACCESS.2016.2647238
3. El-Ghazali, Talbi. (2009). Metaheuristics: From Design to Implementation. https://www.sciencedirect.com/science/article/abs/pii/S0377221709009382
4. https://www.baeldung.com/cs/swarm-intelligence 30th December 2022 (Accessed date)
5. Daniel Angus, Clinton J. Woodward. (2009). Multiple Objective Ant Colony Optimisation. *Swarm Intelligence*, 3(1), 69–85. doi:10.1007/S11721-008-0022-4
6. Xianghua Chu, Teresa Wu, Jeffery D. Weir, Yuhui Shi, Ben Niu, Li Li. (2020). Learning-Interaction-Diversification Framework for Swarm Intelligence Optimizers: A Unified Perspective. *Neural Computing and Applications*, 32(6), 1789–1809. doi:10.1007/S00521-018-3657-0
7. Rabia Korkmaz Tan, Şebnem Bora. (2017). Parameter Tuning in Modeling and Simulations by Using Swarm Intelligence Optimization Algorithms," *2017 9th International Conference on Computational Intelligence and Communication Networks (CICN),* Girne, Northern Cyprus, 2017, pp. 148–152, doi: 10.1109/CICN.2017.8319375

8. Mehrdad Rostami, Kamal Berahmand, Elahe Nasiri, Saman Forouzandeh. (2021). Review of Swarm Intelligence-Based Feature Selection Methods. *Engineering Applications of Artificial Intelligence*, 100, 104210. doi:10.1016/J.ENGAPPAI.2021.104210

9. Liyun Fu, Houyao Zhu, Chengyun Zhang, Haibin Ouyang, Steven Li. (2021). Hybrid Harmony Search Differential Evolution Algorithm. *IEEE Access*, 9, 21532–21555. doi:10.1109/ACCESS.2021.3055530

10. P. Jayalakshmi, S. Sridevi, Sengathir Janakiraman. (2021). A Hybrid Artificial Bee Colony and Harmony Search Algorithm-Based Metahueristic Approach for Efficient Routing in WSNs. *Wireless Personal Communications*, 121(4), 1–17. doi:10.1007/S11277-021-08875-5

11. Hongbo Wang, Cheng-Cheng Fan, Xuyan Tu. (2016). AFSAOCP: A Novel Artificial Fish Swarm Optimization Algorithm Aided by Ocean Current Power. *Applied Intelligence*, 45(4), 992–1007. doi:10.1007/S10489-016-0798-7

12. Diogo Freitas, Luiz Guerreiro Lopes, Fernando Morgado-Dias. (2020). Particle Swarm Optimisation: A Historical Review Up to the Current Developments. *Entropy*, 22(3), 362. doi:10.3390/E22030362

13. Rui Xu, Jie Xu, Donald C. Wunsch. (2012). A Comparison Study of Validity Indices on Swarm-Intelligence-Based Clustering. *IEEE Transactions on Systems, Man, and Cybernetics, Part B*, 42(4), 1243–1256. doi:10.1109/TSMCB.2012.2188509

14. Stephen M. Stigler. (1981). Gauss and the Invention of Least Squares. *Annals of Statistics*, 9(3), 465–474. doi:10.1214/AOS/1176345451

15. R. A. Fisher. (1936). The Use of Multiple Measurements in Taxonomic Problems. *Annals of Human Genetics*, 7(2), 179–188. doi:10.1111/J.1469-1809.1936.TB02137.X

16. P. J. Cheek. (1990). Generalized Linear Models. *Journal of the Royal Statistical Society Series C-Applied Statistics*, 39(3), 385–386. doi:10.2307/2347392

17. Leo Breiman. (1983). Classification and Regression Trees. https://www.taylorfrancis.com/books/mono/10.1201/9781315139470/classification-regression-trees-leo-breiman

18. Loic Yengo, Abdelilah Arredouani, Michel Marre, Ronan Roussel, Martine Vaxillaire, Mario Falchi, Abdelali Haoudi, Jean Tichet, Beverley Balkau, Amélie Bonnefond, Philippe Froguel. (2016). Impact of Statistical Models on the Prediction of Type 2 Diabetes Using Non-Targeted Metabolomics Profiling. *Molecular Metabolism*, 5(10), 918–925. doi:10.1016/J.MOLMET.2016.08.011

19. Charles J. Stone. (1986). The Dimensionality Reduction Principle for Generalized Additive Models. *Annals of Statistics*, 14(2), 590–606. doi:10.1214/AOS/1176349940

20. Geoffrey J. McLachlan. (1992). Discriminant Analysis and Statistical Pattern Recognition. https://www.wiley.com/en-us/Discriminant+Analysis+and+Statistical+Pattern+Recognition-p-9780471691150

21. Karl Pearson. (2010). On the Theory of Contingency. Journal of the American Statistical Association [Internet]. 1930 Sep; 25(171), 320. Available from: http://dx.doi.org/10.2307/2278196.

22. Jerome L. Myers, Arnold D. Well. (1991). Research Design and Statistical Analysis, Third Edition by Jerome L. Myers, Arnold D. Well, Robert F. Lorch, Jr. *International Statistical Review* [Internet]. 2011 Nov 21; 79(3), 491–492. Available from: http://dx.doi.org/10.1111/j.1751-5823.2011.00159_12.x

23. Matthias Greiner, Dirk Pfeiffer, Ronald D. Smith. (2000). Principles and Practical Application of The Receiver-Operating Characteristic Analysis for Diagnostic Tests. *Preventive Veterinary Medicine*, 45(1), 23–41. doi:10.1016/S0167-5877(00)00115-X

3 Data Classification by Decision Trees – An Illustration

3.1 INTRODUCTION

Decision trees are said to be one of the most efficient and scalable algorithms to map data observations about an item to derive conclusions corresponding to the items target value [1]. A decision tree is used to build classification model in the form of a tree-like structure based on certain condition with class-labeled training tuples. The algorithm breaks down the whole dataset into smaller chunks from the root node until the designated leaf node is reached. Each of the internal nodes signifies a test on the attribute and each leaf node signifies the outcome of the test. The selection of the root node is based upon the chosen attribute selection measure [2]. The attribute selection measure may be information gain, gain ratio, or Gini index. In accordance with the evaluation of the selected attributes, the tree uses one of the splitting measures to classify the class-labeled training tuples [3].

Procedure 3.1 Workflow of C4.5 decision tree algorithm

01: **begin**

02: **for** $d = 1$ to number of training observations and its class values

03: **for** $a = 1$ to number of candidate attributes

04: Select a splitting criterion

05: **end for**

06: **end for**

07: Create a node N_d

08: **if** all observations in the training dataset have the same class output value C,
then

09: return N_d as a leaf node labeled with C

10: **if** *attribute list* $= \{\varphi\}$, **then**

11: return N_d as a leaf node labeled with majority class output value.

12: Apply selected splitting criterion

DOI: 10.1201/9781003330189-3

13: Label node N_d with the splitting criterion attribute.

14: Remove the splitting criterion attribute from the attribute list

15: **for** each value i in the splitting criterion attribute

16: D_i = no. of observations in training data satisfying attribute value i.

17: **if** D_i is empty then

18: attach a leaf node labeled with majority value to node N_d

19: **else**

20: attach the node returned by decision tree to node N_d

21: **end if**

22: **end for**

23: return node N_d

24: **end if**

25: **end if**

26: **for** $i = 1$ to number of training tuples (N)

27: **if** Class$_i$ = Predicted Class$_i$ of testing data **then**

28: **if** Class$_i$ = Class label of positive tuples **then**

29: TP = TP + 1

30: **else if** Class$_i$ = Class label of negative tuples **then**

31: TN = TN + 1

32: **end if**

33: **end if**

34: **end for**

35: Fitness function = (TP + TN/N)

36: **end**

3.2 VARIANTS OF DECISION TREES

The evolution of decision tree algorithm has different variants based on the function-ality and parametric evaluation [4]. During the late 1970s, J. Ross Quinlan, one of the researcher in the domain of machine learning, proposed the decision tree algorithm which is said to be as Iterative Dichotomiser (ID3). Later he presented C4.5 which is the successor of ID3 algorithm. The C4.5 decision tree algorithm used for different sorts of applications in order to determine the best split that occurs among the set of input attributes [5]. During the year 1984, a group of statisticians published a book on Classification and Regression Trees (CART), which then completely described about the generation of binary decision trees. These algorithms work well behind the strategy of decision tree induction. The thing is they follow the mechanism of greedy approach in a top-down recursive fashion, following the divide and conquer policy [6].

3.3   DECISION TREES SPLITTING MEASURES

The execution of decision tree depends on the splitting criterion, which specifies how the split has to be made in accordance with the input attributes and the class label is determined. The splitting criterion can be fixed based on the performance of the decision tree algorithm for the observed data [7,8]. The following splitting measures have been investigated for our problem with brief representation (Han & Kamber 2011).

3.3.1   INFORMATION GAIN

The indication to classify a tuple over D is expressed as follows:

$$\text{Info}(D) = -\sum_{i-1}^{m} p_i \log_2(p_i) \tag{3.1}$$

If we have to partition the data tuples in D on the given attribute A having v distinct values, $\{a_1, a_2, a_3, \cdots a_v\}$ as observed from the training data, then the information needed after partitioning is measured by the following equation:

$$\text{Info}_A(D) = \sum_{j-1}^{v} \frac{|D_j|}{|D|} \times \text{Info}(D_j) \tag{3.2}$$

3.3.2   GAIN RATIO

Gain ratio estimates info (D) with split info significance which derived over standardizing the value of info gain. The info (D) is expressed as follows:

$$\text{Split Info}_A(D) = -\sum_{j-1}^{v} \frac{|D_j|}{|D|} \times \log_2\left(\frac{|D_j|}{|D|}\right) \tag{3.3}$$

The gain ratio is defined as follows:

$$\text{Gain Ratio}(A) = \frac{\text{Gain}(A)}{\text{Split Info}(A)} \tag{3.4}$$

3.3.3 GINI INDEX

The impurity over D is processed through Gini index in the following equations:

$$\text{Gini}(D) = 1 - \sum_{i-1}^{m} p_i^2 \qquad (3.5)$$

$$\text{Gini}_A(D) = -\frac{|D_1|}{|D|}\text{Gini}(D_1) + \frac{|D_2|}{|D|}\text{Gini}(D_2) \qquad (3.6)$$

Information gain is probably a good measure, but it is not suitable for the attributes having a larger number of distinct values. Gini index which is an impurity measure-based criterion is suitable for the process of divergence between the target attribute values [9]. It signifies the maximum probability distribution with the target attribute values. Therefore, the attribute selection measure gain ratio is used up for generating the decision tree for data classification.

3.4 EXAMPLE ILLUSTRATION

The following illustration uses information gain as the splitting criterion for the dataset considered. The dataset used for illustration is weather dataset.

The information needed to classify a tuple in D is given by

$$\text{Info}(D) = -\sum_{i=1}^{m} p_i \log_2(p_i) \qquad (3.7)$$

The information required after partitioning is given by

$$\text{Info}_A(D) = \sum_{j=1}^{v} \frac{|D_j|}{|D|} \times \text{Info}(D_j) \qquad (3.8)$$

The weather problem dataset is discussed in most of the machine learning techniques. The dataset describes the condition of whether to play a specified game or not. For a condition to play a specified game, the attributes are defined to conclude a solution whether to play the game or not. Table 3.1 describes the dataset with four attributes and label. The attributes are outlook, temperature, humidity, and wind. The attribute outlook is provided with distributions such as sunny, overcast, and rain. Then, the attribute temperature is distributed as hot, mild, and cool.

The attribute humidity is high or normal; hence, it is of only two distributions and the attribute wind is of the same such as true or false. The label attribute play is provided with class label yes or no, indicating whether the particular game can be played or not. The described dataset is of categorical data rather than numerical.

TABLE 3.1
Dataset Description

S. No.	Outlook	Temperature	Humidity	Wind	Play
1	Sunny	Hot	High	False	No
2	Sunny	Hot	High	True	No
3	Overcast	Hot	High	False	Yes
4	Rain	Mild	High	False	Yes
5	Rain	Cool	Normal	False	Yes
6	Rain	Cool	Normal	True	No
7	Overcast	Cool	Normal	True	Yes
8	Sunny	Mild	High	False	No
9	Sunny	Cool	Normal	False	Yes
10	Rainy	Mild	Normal	False	Yes
11	Sunny	Mild	Normal	True	Yes
12	Overcast	Mild	High	True	Yes
13	Overcast	Hot	Normal	False	Yes
14	Rainy	Mild	High	True	No

The class-labeled attribute has two distinct values (namely, {yes, no}). There are nine tuples of class yes and five tuples of class no. To find the splitting criterion for these tuples, we must compute the information gain of each attribute. The information needed to classify a tuple in D is computed using equation (3.7):

$$\text{Info}(D) = -\frac{9}{14}\log_2(\frac{9}{14}) - \frac{5}{14}\log_2(\frac{5}{14})$$

$$= (-0.6428 * -0.6375) * (-0.3571 * -1.4855)$$

$$= 0.940 \text{ bits}$$

Next, we need to compute the information gain requirement for each attribute. Let's start with attribute outlook. Looking at the distribution of yes and no tuples for each distribution of the attribute outlook, there are three distributions: sunny, overcast, and rain. For the outlook category sunny, there are two yes and three no tuples. For the category overcast, there are four yes tuples and zero no tuples. For the category rain, there are three yes tuples and two no tuples. Using equation (3.8), the information needed which is made according to the attribute outlook is

$$\text{Info}_{\text{outlook}}(D) = (\frac{5}{14} \times (-\frac{2}{5}\log_2(\frac{2}{5}) - \frac{3}{5}\log_2(\frac{3}{5})))$$

$$+ (\frac{4}{14} \times (-\frac{4}{4}\log_2(\frac{4}{4}) - \frac{0}{4}\log_2(\frac{0}{4})))$$

$$+ (\frac{5}{14} \times (-\frac{3}{5}\log_2(\frac{3}{5}) - \frac{2}{5}\log_2(\frac{2}{5})))$$

$$= 0.3466 + 0.3466$$

$$= 0.6932 \text{ bits.}$$

Therefore, the gain in information for the partition outlook is

$$\text{Gain(outlook)} = \text{Info}(D) - \text{Info}_{\text{outlook}}(D)$$

$$= 0.940 - 0.6932$$

$$= 0.2468 \text{ bits.}$$

The expected information gain made according to the attribute temperature is

$$\text{Info}_{\text{temperature}}(D) = (\frac{4}{14} \times (-\frac{2}{4} \log_2(\frac{2}{4}) - \frac{2}{4} \log_2(\frac{2}{4})))$$

$$+ (\frac{6}{14} \times (-\frac{4}{6} \log_2(\frac{4}{6}) - \frac{2}{6} \log_2(\frac{2}{6})))$$

$$+ (\frac{4}{14} \times (-\frac{3}{4} \log_2(\frac{3}{4}) - \frac{1}{4} \log_2(\frac{1}{4})))$$

$$= 0.2857 + 0.3940 + 0.2318$$

$$= 0.9115 \text{ bits.}$$

Therefore, the gain in information for the partition temperature is

$$\text{Gain(temperature)} = \text{Info}(D) - \text{Info}_{\text{temperature}}(D)$$

$$= 0.940 - 0.9115$$

$$= 0.0285 \text{ bits.}$$

The information gain made according to the attribute humidity is

$$\text{Info}_{\text{humidity}}(D) = (\frac{7}{14} \times (-\frac{3}{7} \log_2(\frac{3}{7}) - \frac{4}{7} \log_2(\frac{4}{7})))$$

$$+ (\frac{7}{14} \times (-\frac{6}{7} \log_2(\frac{6}{7}) - \frac{1}{7} \log_2(\frac{1}{7})))$$

$$= 0.4925 + 0.2957$$

$$= 0.7882 \text{ bits.}$$

Therefore, the gain in information for the partition humidity is

$$\text{Gain(humidity)} = \text{Info}(D) - \text{Info}_{\text{humidity}}(D)$$

$$= 0.940 - 0.7882$$

$$= 0.1518 \text{ bits.}$$

The information gain made according to the attribute wind is

$$\text{Info}_{\text{humidity}}(D) = (\frac{8}{14} \times (-\frac{6}{8}\log_2(\frac{6}{8}) - \frac{2}{8}\log_2(\frac{2}{8})))$$

$$+ (\frac{6}{14} \times (-\frac{3}{6}\log_2(\frac{3}{6}) - \frac{3}{6}\log_2(\frac{3}{6})))$$

$$= 0.4635 + 0.4285$$

$$= 0.892 \text{ bits.}$$

Therefore, the gain in information for the partition wind is

$$\text{Gain(wind)} = \text{Info}(D) - \text{Info}_{\text{wind}}(D)$$

$$= 0.940 - 0.892$$

$$= 0.048 \text{ bits.}$$

Among all of the attributes, the attribute outlook has the highest information gain and it is selected as the splitting attribute. The node N is labeled with outlook and all the branches are distributed for the attribute values accordingly as shown in Figure 3.1.

For the distribution of the attribute outlook, which is overcast, the end of this branch is labeled with yes. Then, the attribute with the highest gain value next to outlook is humidity looking at the distribution of the attribute that is of high and normal. Proceeding with the distribution outlook is sunny in Figure 3.2, and if humidity is high, then the end of this branch is labeled with No else; if humidity is of normal, then the end of this branch is labeled with yes.

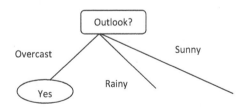

FIGURE 3.1   Decision tree generation stage 1.

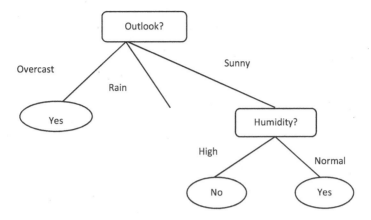

FIGURE 3.2 Decision tree generation stage 2.

Then, the attribute with highest gain next to outlook and humidity is wind. For the distribution, if the outlook is rainy and the attribute wind is said to be false, then the end of the node is labeled with yes as shown in Figure 3.3; otherwise, if wind is said to be true, then the end of the node is labeled with No, and the final tree is constructed accordingly.

3.4.1 GAIN RATIO

The split information obtained by means of gain ratio with Info (D) is

$$\text{Split Info}_A(D) = -\sum_{j=1}^{v} \frac{|D_j|}{|D|} \times \log_2\left(\frac{|D_j|}{|D|}\right) \tag{3.9}$$

The gain ratio is defined as

$$\text{Gain Ratio}(A) = \frac{\text{Gain}(A)}{\text{Split Info}(A)} \tag{3.10}$$

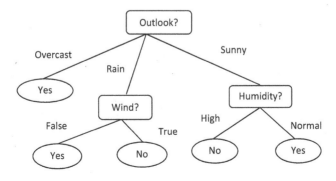

FIGURE 3.3 Decision tree generation stage 3.

Using Table 3.1, the split information value for the attribute outlook is calculated as follows:

$$\text{Split Info}_{\text{outlook}}(D) = -\frac{5}{14} \times \log_2\left(\frac{5}{14}\right) - \frac{4}{14} \times \log_2\left(\frac{4}{14}\right) - \frac{5}{14} \times \log_2\left(\frac{5}{14}\right)$$

$$= 0.5304 + 0.5163 + 0.5304$$

$$= 1.5771$$

The gain ratio of the attribute outlook is calculated as follows:

$$\text{Gain Ratio(outlook)} = \frac{0.2468}{1.5771}$$

$$= 0.1564$$

For the attribute temperature, it has three distributions such as hot, mild, and cool; hence, the split information of the attribute temperature is

$$\text{Split Info}_{\text{temperature}}(D) = -\frac{4}{14} \times \log_2\left(\frac{4}{14}\right) - \frac{6}{14} \times \log_2\left(\frac{6}{14}\right) - \frac{4}{14} \times \log_2\left(\frac{4}{14}\right)$$

$$= 0.5163 + 0.5238 + 0.5163$$

$$= 1.5564$$

The gain ratio of the attribute temperature is calculated as follows:

$$\text{Gain Ratio(temperature)} = \frac{0.0285}{1.5564}$$

$$= 0.0183$$

For the attribute humidity, it has two distributions namely high and normal. The split information for the attribute humidity is

$$\text{Split Info}_{\text{humidity}}(D) = -\frac{7}{14} \times \log_2\left(\frac{7}{14}\right) - \frac{7}{14} \times \log_2\left(\frac{7}{14}\right)$$

$$= 0.5 + 0.5$$

$$= 1.0$$

The gain ratio of the attribute humidity is calculated as follows:

$$\text{Gain Ratio(humidity)} = \frac{0.1518}{1.0}$$

$$= 0.1518$$

Similarly, the split information of the attribute wind is

$$\text{Split Info}_{\text{wind}}(D) = -\frac{8}{14} \times \log_2\left(\frac{8}{14}\right) - \frac{6}{14} \times \log_2\left(\frac{6}{14}\right)$$

$$= 0.4613 + 0.5238$$

$$= 0.9851$$

The gain ratio of the attribute wind is calculated as follows:

$$\text{Gain Ratio(wind)} = \frac{0.0480}{0.9851}$$

$$= 0.0487$$

From the computed values of gain ratio of all the attributes the attribute outlook has the highest gain when compared to other such attributes. Therefore, for the construction of the tree, the root node N is outlook from which the other node originates. Figure 3.4 signifies the root node outlook with its distributions.

For the first distribution in the attribute outlook, if outlook is overcast, then the prediction is yes. The attribute next to outlook which has the highest gain ratio is humidity; hence, it is chosen as the next node in constructing the tree. From Figure 3.5, we can observe that if outlook is sunny and humidity is high, then the label is yes. If the attribute outlook is sunny and humidity is normal, then the label is no.

Then, the next attribute which has the highest gain ratio is wind. Figure 3.6 depicts that if outlook is rainy and wind is false, then the label is yes, and if the attribute outlook is rainy and the attribute wind is true, then the label is no. Therefore, the tree ends up with this because there occurs no such further splitting in the attribute.

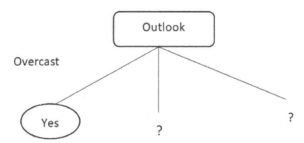

FIGURE 3.4 Decision tree generation stage 1.

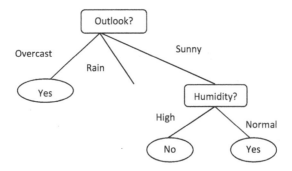

FIGURE 3.5   Decision tree generation stage 2.

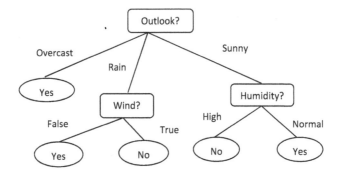

FIGURE 3.6   Decision tree generation stage 3.

3.4.2   GINI INDEX

The impurity in a partition using Gini index is calculated as follows:

$$\text{Gini}(D) = 1 - \sum_{i=1}^{m} p_i^2 \tag{3.11}$$

The Gini index for a partition is given as follows:

$$\text{Gini}_A(D) = \frac{|D_1|}{|D|}\text{Gini}(D_1) + \frac{|D_2|}{|D|}\text{Gini}(D_2) \tag{3.12}$$

Consider the dataset of Table 4.1 which contains nine tuples belonging to the class play = Yes and five tuples belonging to the class play = No. The impurity in the dataset D with respect to Gini index is calculated using the following equation:

$$\text{Gini}(D) = 1 - \left(\frac{9}{14}\right)^2 - \left(\frac{5}{14}\right)^2$$

$$= 0.4593$$

To find the splitting criterion for the tuples in D, we have to compute the Gini index for each attribute. From Table 3.1, the attribute outlook has three distributions such as sunny, overcast, and rain. Consider each possible splitting subsets for the above distributions: {overcast}, {sunny}, {rain}, {overcast, sunny}, {sunny, rain}, and {overcast, rain}. Consider the subset {overcast, sunny}. This would result in nine tuples in partition D_1 satisfying the condition 'outlook $\in$ {overcast, sunny}'. The remaining five tuples of D will be assigned to partition D_2. The Gini index value computed based on this partitioning is

$\text{Gini}_{\text{outlook}\in\{\text{overcast, sunny}\}}(D)$

$$= \frac{9}{14}\text{Gini}(D_1) + \frac{5}{14}\text{Gini}(D_2)$$

$$= \frac{9}{14}\left(1 - \left(\frac{6}{9}\right)^2 - \left(\frac{3}{9}\right)^2\right) + \frac{5}{14}\left(1 - \left(\frac{3}{5}\right)^2 - \left(\frac{2}{5}\right)^2\right)$$

$$= 0.2857 + 0.1714$$

$$= 0.4572$$

Next, for the subset {sunny, rainy},

$\text{Gini}_{\text{outlook}\in\{\text{sunny, rainy}\}}(D)$

$$= \frac{10}{14}\text{Gini}(D_1) + \frac{4}{14}\text{Gini}(D_2)$$

$$= \frac{10}{14}\left(1 - \left(\frac{5}{10}\right)^2 - \left(\frac{5}{10}\right)^2\right) + \frac{4}{14}\left(1 - \left(\frac{4}{4}\right)^2 - \left(\frac{0}{4}\right)^2\right)$$

$$= 0.3572$$

Next, for the subset {overcast, rainy}, the computation of Gini value is

$\text{Gini}_{\text{outlook}\in\{\text{overcast, rainy}\}}(D)$

$$= \frac{9}{14}\text{Gini}(D_1) + \frac{5}{14}\text{Gini}(D_2)$$

$$= \frac{9}{14}\left(1 - \left(\frac{7}{9}\right)^2 - \left(\frac{2}{9}\right)^2\right) + \frac{5}{14}\left(1 - \left(\frac{2}{5}\right)^2 - \left(\frac{3}{5}\right)^2\right)$$

$$= 0.2222 + 0.1714$$

$$= 0.3936$$

The Gini value for outlook= {overcast} is

$\text{Gini}_{\text{outlook} \in \{\text{overcast}\}}(D)$

$$= \frac{4}{14}\text{Gini}(D_1) + \frac{10}{14}\text{Gini}(D_2)$$

$$= \frac{4}{14}\left(1 - \left(\frac{4}{4}\right)^2 - \left(\frac{0}{4}\right)^2\right) + \frac{10}{14}\left(1 - \left(\frac{5}{10}\right)^2 - \left(\frac{5}{10}\right)^2\right)$$

$$= 0.3572$$

The Gini value for outlook = {sunny} is

$\text{Gini}_{\text{outlook} \in \{\text{sunny}\}}(D)$

$$= \frac{5}{14}\text{Gini}(D_1) + \frac{9}{14}\text{Gini}(D_2)$$

$$= \frac{5}{14}\left(1 - \left(\frac{2}{5}\right)^2 - \left(\frac{3}{5}\right)^2\right) + \frac{9}{14}\left(1 - \left(\frac{7}{9}\right)^2 - \left(\frac{2}{9}\right)^2\right)$$

$$= 0.1714 + 0.2222$$

$$= 0.3936$$

The Gini value for outlook = {rain} is

$\text{Gini}_{\text{outlook} \in \{\text{rain}\}}(D)$

$$= \frac{5}{14}\text{Gini}(D_1) + \frac{9}{14}\text{Gini}(D_2)$$

$$= \frac{5}{14}\left(1 - \left(\frac{3}{5}\right)^2 - \left(\frac{2}{5}\right)^2\right) + \frac{9}{14}\left(1 - \left(\frac{6}{9}\right)^2 - \left(\frac{3}{9}\right)^2\right)$$

$$= 0.1714 + 0.2857$$

$$= 0.4572$$

Consider the next attribute temperature where the distribution for the attribute temperature is hot, mild, and cool. Each possible splitting subset for the above distributions is {hot}, {mild}, {cool}, {hot, mild}, {mild, cool}, and {hot, cool}. The evaluation of the Gini values for each of the subset is as follows:

i. $\text{Gini}_{temperature \in \{mild\}}(D)$

$$= \frac{6}{14}\text{Gini}(D_1) + \frac{8}{14}\text{Gini}(D_2)$$

$$= \frac{6}{14}\left(1 - \left(\frac{4}{6}\right)^2 - \left(\frac{2}{6}\right)^2\right) + \frac{8}{14}\left(1 - \left(\frac{5}{8}\right)^2 - \left(\frac{3}{8}\right)^2\right)$$

$$= 0.1897 + 0.2679$$

$$= 0.4576$$

ii. $\text{Gini}_{temperature \in \{hot\}}(D)$

$$= \frac{4}{14}\text{Gini}(D_1) + \frac{10}{14}\text{Gini}(D_2)$$

$$= \frac{4}{14}\left(1 - \left(\frac{2}{4}\right)^2 - \left(\frac{2}{4}\right)^2\right) + \frac{10}{14}\left(1 - \left(\frac{7}{10}\right)^2 - \left(\frac{3}{10}\right)^2\right)$$

$$= 0.1429 + 0.3000$$

$$= 0.4429$$

iii. $\text{Gini}_{temperature \in \{cool\}}(D)$

$$= \frac{4}{14}\text{Gini}(D_1) + \frac{10}{14}\text{Gini}(D_2)$$

$$= \frac{4}{14}\left(1 - \left(\frac{3}{4}\right)^2 - \left(\frac{1}{4}\right)^2\right) + \frac{10}{14}\left(1 - \left(\frac{6}{10}\right)^2 - \left(\frac{4}{10}\right)^2\right)$$

$$= 0.1071 + 0.3429$$

$$= 0.4499$$

iv. $\text{Gini}_{\text{temperature}\in\{\text{mild, hot}\}}(D)$

$$= \frac{10}{14}\text{Gini}(D_1) + \frac{4}{14}\text{Gini}(D_2)$$

$$= \frac{10}{14}\left(1 - \left(\frac{6}{10}\right)^2 - \left(\frac{4}{10}\right)^2\right) + \frac{4}{14}\left(1 - \left(\frac{3}{4}\right)^2 - \left(\frac{1}{4}\right)^2\right)$$

$$= 0.3429 + 0.1071$$

$$= 0.4499$$

v. $\text{Gini}_{\text{temperature}\in\{\text{hot, cool}\}}(D)$

$$= \frac{8}{14}\text{Gini}(D_1) + \frac{6}{14}\text{Gini}(D_2)$$

$$= \frac{8}{14}\left(1 - \left(\frac{5}{8}\right)^2 - \left(\frac{3}{8}\right)^2\right) + \frac{6}{14}\left(1 - \left(\frac{4}{6}\right)^2 - \left(\frac{2}{6}\right)^2\right)$$

$$= 0.2679 + 0.1897$$

$$= 0.4576$$

vi. $\text{Gini}_{\text{temperature}\in\{\text{mild, cool}\}}(D)$

$$= \frac{10}{14}\text{Gini}(D_1) + \frac{4}{14}\text{Gini}(D_2)$$

$$= 0.3000 + 0.1429$$

$$= 0.4429$$

Consider the next attribute humidity where the distribution for the attribute humidity is high and normal. Each possible splitting subset for the above distributions is {high}, {normal}, and {high, normal}. The evaluation of the Gini values for each of the subsets is as follows:

vii. $\text{Gini}_{\text{humidity}\in\{\text{high}\}}(D)$

$$= \frac{7}{14}\text{Gini}(D_1) + \frac{7}{14}\text{Gini}(D_2)$$

$$= \frac{7}{14}\left(1-\left(\frac{4}{7}\right)^2-\left(\frac{3}{7}\right)^2\right)+\frac{7}{14}\left(1-\left(\frac{6}{7}\right)^2-\left(\frac{1}{7}\right)^2\right)$$

$$= 0.2450+0.1225$$

$$= 0.3674$$

viii. $Gini_{humidity \in \{normal\}}(D)$

$$= \frac{7}{14}Gini(D_1)+\frac{7}{14}Gini(D_2)$$

$$= \frac{7}{14}\left(1-\left(\frac{6}{7}\right)^2-\left(\frac{1}{7}\right)^2\right)+\frac{7}{14}\left(1-\left(\frac{4}{7}\right)^2-\left(\frac{3}{7}\right)^2\right)$$

$$= 0.1225+0.2450$$

$$= 0.3674$$

ix. $Gini_{humidity \in \{high,\ normal\}}(D)$

$$= \frac{14}{14}Gini(D_1)+\frac{0}{14}Gini(D_2)$$

$$= \frac{14}{14}\left(1-\left(\frac{10}{14}\right)^2-\left(\frac{4}{14}\right)^2\right)$$

$$= 0.4083$$

Consider the next attribute wind where the distribution for the attribute wind is true and false. Each possible splitting subset for the above distributions is {true}, {false}, and {true, false}. The evaluation of the Gini values for each of the subset is as follows:

x. $Gini_{wind \in \{true\}}(D)$

$$= \frac{6}{14}Gini(D_1)+\frac{8}{14}Gini(D_2)$$

$$= \frac{6}{14}\left(1-\left(\frac{3}{6}\right)^2-\left(\frac{3}{6}\right)^2\right)+\frac{8}{14}\left(1-\left(\frac{6}{8}\right)^2-\left(\frac{2}{8}\right)^2\right)$$

$$= 0.2143+0.2143$$

$$= 0.4268$$

xi. $\text{Gini}_{\text{wind}\in\{\text{false}\}}(D)$

$$= \frac{8}{14}\text{Gini}(D_1) + \frac{6}{14}\text{Gini}(D_2)$$

$$= \frac{8}{14}\left(1 - \left(\frac{6}{8}\right)^2 - \left(\frac{2}{8}\right)^2\right) + \frac{6}{14}\left(1 - \left(\frac{3}{6}\right)^2 - \left(\frac{3}{6}\right)^2\right)$$

$$= 0.2143 + 0.2143$$

$$= 0.4268$$

xii. $\text{Gini}_{\text{wind}\in\{\text{true, false}\}}(D)$

$$= \frac{14}{14}\text{Gini}(D_1) + \frac{0}{14}\text{Gini}(D_2)$$

$$= \frac{14}{14}\left(1 - \left(\frac{9}{14}\right)^2 - \left(\frac{5}{14}\right)^2\right)$$

$$= 0.4593$$

After computing the gain for all the attributes with their subsets, we have to compute the subset for all of the attributes with reduction in impurity. Among all the attributes, the attribute with subsets that have minimum Gini value is outlook with its subsets with minimum Gini value that is {overcast} and {sunny, rain} with a value of 0.3572 and the reduction in impurity of 0.4593 − 0.3572 = 0.1021. Therefore, the root node N is selected to be outlook with its distributions as shown in Figure 3.7, and the next attribute with reduction in impurity is chosen to be humidity with its subsets as {high} and {normal}. The reduced Gini value chosen by this subset is 0.3674 and the impurity level is calculated as 0.4593 − 0.3674 = 0.0919.

Therefore, the attribute humidity is chosen for the next split with its distribution high and normal. Figure 3.8 describes the next level for the split made according to the attribute humidity.

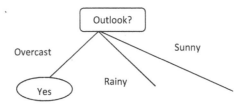

FIGURE 3.7   Decision tree generation stage 1.

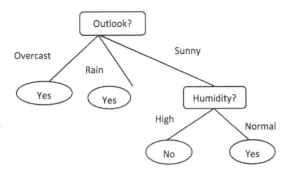

FIGURE 3.8 Decision tree generation stage 2.

Hence, for each category of splitting criterion, the tree gets generated accordingly. In the case of larger datasets, the generation of tree may vary and become complex to visualize under those circumstances where the phenomenon of pre-pruning and post-pruning can be made considering the important branches to functionalize. This will eliminate the process of over-fitting that occurs in larger datasets.

3.5 APPLICATIONS

The utilization of decision trees has been reported majorly for the cases corresponding to data classification and prediction. It is widely used in different sorts of applications for both discrete and continuous valued attributes [10]. Recently, in medical informatics, the utilization of decision trees has become popular in accordance with medical data analysis [11]. Example cases focusing on diagnosing the medical condition of patient group explicitly reveal the pattern of symptoms, analyzing clinical subtypes and risk factor analysis in medical data.

REFERENCES

1. Steven L. Salzberg. (1994). Book Review: C4.5: Programs for Machine Learning by J. Ross Quinlan. Morgan Kaufmann Publishers, Inc., 1993. *Machine Learning*, 16(3), 235–240. doi:10.1023/A:1022645310020
2. Steven L. Salzberg. (1994). C4.5: Programs for Machine Learning by J. Ross Quinlan. Morgan Kaufmann Publishers, Inc., 1993. *Machine Learning*, 16(3), 235–240. doi:10.1007/BF00993309
3. Ian M. Carter. (1989). Application of Expert Systems: J Ross Quinlan Addison-Wesley, 1987, Hardback, 223 pp £19.95, ISBN: 0 201 17449 9. *Artificial Intelligence in Engineering*, 4(1), 54. doi:10.1016/0954-1810(89)90025-3
4. Jan Bogaert, Reinhart Ceulemans, David Salvador-Van Eysenrode. (2004). Decision Tree Algorithm for Detection of Spatial Processes in Landscape Transformation. *Environmental Management*, 33(1), 62–73. doi:10.1007/S00267-003-0027-0
5. Wei Liu, Sanjay Chawla, David A. Cieslak, Nitesh V. Chawla. (2010). A Robust Decision Tree Algorithm for Imbalanced Data Sets. *Proceedings of the 2010 SIAM International Conference on Data Mining* [Internet]. 2010 Apr 29. doi:10.1137/1.9781611972801.67

6. Wei Dai, Wei Ji. (2014). A MapReduce Implementation of C4.5 Decision Tree Algorithm. *International Journal of Database Theory and Application*, 7(1), 49–60. doi:10.14257/IJDTA.2014.7.1.05

7. Yan Yan Song, Ying Lu. (2015). Decision Tree Methods: Applications for Classification and Prediction. *Shanghai Archives of Psychiatry*, 27(2), 130–135. doi:10.11919/J. ISSN.1002-0829.215044

8. Mahesh Pal, Paul M. Mather. (2003). An Assessment of the Effectiveness of Decision Tree Methods for Land Cover Classification. *Remote Sensing of Environment*, 86(4), 554–565. doi:10.1016/S0034-4257(03)00132-9

9. A. S. Abdullah. (2022). Assessment of the Risk Factors of Type II Diabetes Using ACO with Self-Regulative Update Function and Decision Trees by Evaluation from Fisher's Z-Transformation. *Medical & Biological Engineering & Computing*, 60(5), 1391–1415. doi:10.1007/s11517-022-02530-2

10. A. S. Abdullah. (2022). Assessment of Risk Factors in Medical Data Using Improved Binary Artificial Fish Swarm Algorithm with Classification Upon Evaluation from F-Test. *International Journal of Swarm Intelligence research*, 13(1), 1–26. doi:10.4018/IJSIR.2022010105

11. A. S. Abdullah, S. Selvakumar, M. Venkatesh. (2021). Assessment and Evaluation of CHD Risk Factors Using Weighted Ranked Correlation and Regression With Data Classification. *Methodologies and Application*, 25(6), 4979–5001. doi:10.1007/S00500-021-05663-Y

4 Predictive Analytics Using Ant Colony Optimization with Decision Trees for Medical Data

4.1 DATA PRE-PROCESSING

Datasets corresponding to CHD, cancer, retinopathy, type II diabetes, and Pima Indian diabetic dataset have been used for experimentation as described in Section 1.9. The observed data have been pre-processed according to the stages in data cleaning, transformation, and preparation [1]. The major consequence is to determine the risk factors across a region for the real-world dataset in order to make a region-based analysis. The repository dataset has also been used to fix the efficacy of the proposed algorithmic model. The collected data consist of both categorical and continuous values. Before moving up to the training phase, the data have to be prepared in a uniform format to a given specified range. All the representations are made in accordance with the numerical format that best suits the training of the model. To make the data into a specified interval of representation, data normalization has been used over the processed dataset. There are about three forms of data normalization such as min-max, Z-score, and normalization by decimal scaling. The mechanism to handle numeric data values relies on min-max with range zero or Z-score technique. In this method, normalization is made in the following equation:

$$Z = \frac{X_i - \mu}{\sigma} \qquad (4.1)$$

where X_i is the value of attribute A, μ is the mean value, and σ is the standard deviation.

Once the data have been normalized, they are ready to be used for training the feature set associated with the collected data.

4.2 ACO – DECISION TREES

ACO is one of the meta-heuristic methods that are intended for finding the best path for a given weighted graph of input. The most important feature in ACO is the mechanism of learning intended through the social behavior in a collective fashion.

The selection of the shortest path is the minimal form of feature, set through social interaction among the generated ants. Biological scientists have proved the process of communication among the ants through a substance called pheromones. These pheromones are responsible for the communication and social learning among the ant groups [2].

In fact, ACO is considered to be one among the most successful and widely recognized techniques which exploits the behavior of ants. The ants associated with the ACO algorithm develops solutions by randomly traversing through the given graph, which is accelerated through the pheromone of the model associated along with the edges in the graph. The values of the edges are updated accordingly with respect to the parametric components in run-time by the ants [3]. The decision for updating parametric values depends upon the following factors known to be trails and attractiveness. These parameters make the ants to move their position in order to make a good solution upon increments. In addition to these two parameters, there are two more mechanisms known as trial evaporation and daemon actions. So, based upon the fixation of these parametric values, the optimal decision with the ACO algorithm can be made in a good fashion [4].

Once the features are selected with the ACO algorithm, it is then fed as an input to the decision trees for fitness evaluation. Decision trees have many variants that are applicable for different sorts of applications [5]. Among all the variants of decision tree algorithm C4.5 (J48), decision tree, which is also termed to be the Java execution of C4.5 decision tree algorithm, is used for determining the best combination of risk factors based on the parametric values of the decision tree algorithm.

4.2.1 ACO Pheromone Initialization

The process of pheromone value initialization depends on the intensity of each of the pheromone value during iteration. The set of relevance value is used to fix the intensity of the pheromones at each step [6]. Moreover, a function called soft max scaling function is used to fix the strategy of normalization for the relevance matrix to a scale of $[0-1]$. The search space reduction is made compact by the process of relevance-based criterion during the initialization process [7]. The relevance matrix is generated based upon the number of features used for the dataset during experimentation. The relevance and the similarity matrix play a significant role upon initialization of a number of features in the observed medical data.

4.2.2 Generate Population

The generation of population with ACO depends upon the number of features that has to be fed as input for the algorithmic model. Once the relevance and the similarity matrix are generated, the initial level of the population can be ascertained in accordance with the parametric scale of the model [8]. The fixation of population varies in accordance with the dataset that has to be used for experimentation. So, based upon the nature and number of features corresponding to the dataset, the initial population is generated, which has to be aligned with the relevance and the similarity matrix for the input data [3].

4.2.3 Select Features According to State Transition Rule

During the evolution stage, the ant traverses with the probabilistic level of state transition rule. The ant which is at the position k located over the feature F_i selects the next feature F_j according to the following equation:

$$j = \arg\max_{u \in j_i^k} \left\{ [\tau_u][\eta_1(F_u)]^\alpha [\eta_2(F_i, F_u)]^\beta \right\}.$$ (4.2)

The above equation is operated under the condition only if $q < q_0$, where j_i^k corresponds to the set of unvisited features, τ_u represents the intensity of the pheromone value allied with the feature F_u, and $\eta_1(F_u)$ represents the relevance matrix value associated with the feature F_u

The parameters α and β correspond to updating of pheromones with regard to η_1 and η_2 in relation to heuristic function values. Also, the value of q signifies the randomly generated value and q_0 corresponds to the parametric value of constant in nature. When considering the selection of feature values in a probabilistic rule of occurrence, the ant searches for the best feature in accordance with the following equation:

$$P_k(i,j) = \begin{cases} \dfrac{[\tau_j][\eta_1(F_j)]^\alpha [\eta_2(F_i, F_j)]^\beta}{\sum_{u \in j_i^k} \tau_u [\eta_1(F_u)]^\alpha [\eta_2(F_i, F_u)]^\beta} & j \in j_i^k \\ \\ 0 & \text{otherwise} \end{cases}$$ (4.3)

With this consideration, the search space gets exploited by the ants with regard to the relevance value, and the value of $\alpha = 0$ is set for the relevance matrix. However, the value of the relevance matrix is not signified with the movement of the ants [9].

4.2.4 Pheromone Updating Using Update Rule

Once the traversal of the ants gets accomplished in association with the pheromone value, the corresponding pheromone values of the associated feature get updated according to the following equation:

$$\tau_i(t+1) = (1-\rho)\tau_i(t) + \frac{FC_i}{\sum_{j=1}^{n} FC(j)}$$ (4.4)

The values $\tau_i(t)$ and $\tau_i(t+1)$ represent the quantity of pheromone deposited over the features at a time interval t and $t+1$, respectively. Meanwhile, the values FC_i and FC_j represent the counter value corresponding to that of the feature set F_i.

4.2.5 Sort Features According to Pheromone Values

The features got accelerated with the updating of the pheromone values made by the ants at each interval relative to the time period t and $t+1$. Each of the features is made with the modification in the pheromone values in accordance with the state transition rule and pheromone updating policy. When sorting the set of features, the similarity that exists among the features has to be noted more specifically, or else it may lead to poor accuracy values [10].

Consider an example scenario in which an ant is at the position of feature F_1 which is in a situation to select two additional features out of F_2, F_3, and F_4. If all the features comprise the same pheromone values during selection, then the ant selects its next consequent feature in the same way as that of greedy approach in which the ant selects the features F_2 and F_3. Hence, following the state transition rule, the ant selects the features and then terminates to its position. Hence, according to the policy of selection criterion, the selected features are said to be redundant, and it is suggested that one among them has to be selected [11].

In order to overcome this problem of selecting the features, a measure of feature with a low similarity value is added when selecting the next set of features. Consider the following scenario: the ant is at position of F_1, and the ant is supposed to select the feature upon considering the greedy approach in addition to the feature having the lower similarity measure. Therefore, it has to select among the features F_2, F_3, and F_4 respectively. Hence, following the greedy technique, the ant selects the consequent feature F_2. Then, based upon the measure of low similarity, the ant selects the remaining set of features F_3 and F_4. The feature F_3 has a similarity measure of 0.76 and F_4 has a similarity measure of 0.82 respectively. Then, based upon the lower similarity value, the ant selects the feature F_3, and therefore, the set of selected features is $\{F_1, F_2, F_3\}$ respectively. Thus, the feature set is sorted in accordance with the similarity measure with the pheromone values.

4.2.6 Build Feature Set with Top Pheromone Values

In considering the average measure of similarity, the kth ant selects the feature F_{m-1}^k on an average while traversing its position [12]. Then, the strategy is to assign a new heuristic value for the features that have been unvisited during the traversal. This can be updated by assigning the new information using the following equation:

$$\eta_2(F_j) = \frac{1}{\left[\frac{1}{m-1}\right] \sum\limits_{F_z \in F_{m-1}^k} \text{sim}(F_j, F_z)}, F_j \in X - F_{m-1}^k \tag{4.5}$$

Therefore, the heuristic information gets updated in accordance with the search process by the ants with pheromone values. Hence, the anticipated values of the pheromones and the corresponding feature are selected for the evaluation of the fitness function. The graphical representation of the search space is depicted in Figure 4.1. In the figure, the value of $S_{i,j}$ represents the similarity measure among the features F_i, F_j, and r_i signifies the relevance value.

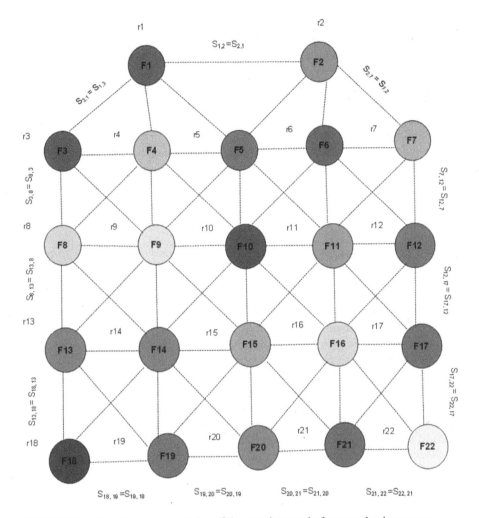

FIGURE 4.1 Graphical representation of the search space in feature selection process.

4.2.7 ACO – DECISION TREE ALGORITHM WORKING PROCEDURE

A colony of ants is a set of asynchronous agents for a given search space. The ants accelerate in accordance with the stochastic local optima policy based on the parameters known to be the trials and attractiveness. The ant, during the execution phase, completes the solution with the modification in the trial value and the value corresponding to the pheromone will provide guidance for the forthcoming ants. Also, the mechanism of trial evaporation and daemon actions are considered to be the decision parameters over the movement of ants [13].

The process of trial evaporation makes the trial values to get decreased so as to avoid unlimited accumulation of trials during process [14]. The process of daemon actions is used to perform centralized actions which can be accomplished by a group of ants [15]. The centralized action is the mechanism to update the global information so as to decide upon the bias during the search process in a non-local perspective. The level of increase or decrease in the level of trial value results in the terminating condition with an improved or reduced level of solution for the given search space [16].

From the selected features by the ACO algorithm, the fitness function is evaluated using Java execution of C4.5 decision tree algorithm. Figure 4.2 depicts the proposed methodological workflow using ACO – Decision tree algorithm. Decision tree algorithm can be evaluated using different splitting criterion measures such as information gain, gain ratio, and Gini index. In this evaluation process, the decision tree algorithm is modeled using gain ratio as the splitting measure. Since gain ratio has the ability to bias the decision tree against the evaluation of the training attributes with larger separate values, it overcomes the problem against other splitting measures.

4.2.8   Cross-Validation

Cross-validation of the medical data is made using *k-fold* cross-validation. In this process, first, the dataset which is labeled is partitioned randomly into *k-equal* subset of data uniformly. Among all the subset of data, one of the subsets is chosen to be the test set, while the remaining $k-1$ subsets are used to train the data model. The set of process is repeated with different cases for test data. Hence, each of the records is used up for the training phase at least once [17].

In this research problem, we have examined all possible cases of cross-validation and the one that is fine-tuned with the medical data is the *10-fold* cross-validation. With this mechanism of cross-validation scheme, the decision support model can achieve relatively good performance with all the tuples of record in the observed medical data. It has also been suggested that, for many of the practical implications, *10-fold* cross-validation is the best choice for evaluating the dataset [18].

4.2.9   Evaluate Fitness for Selected Features Using Decision Trees

The process of fitness evaluation is made using Java execution of C4.5 decision tree algorithm. Once the training and the test data are prepared by *10-fold* cross-validation, they are evaluated for fitness value generation and moved up with the parameters concerned with the ACO algorithm. The algorithm terminating criterion is made with the following conditions:

- Once the stopping criterion is met with the fitness value
- Number of iterations

If the fitness function is reached to the desired level of attainment, then the algorithm gets stopped; otherwise, the algorithm iterates until the stopping criterion is reached. The following pseudo code describes the complete structure of ACO – decision tree algorithm and its process. The proposed model is shown in Procedure 4.1:

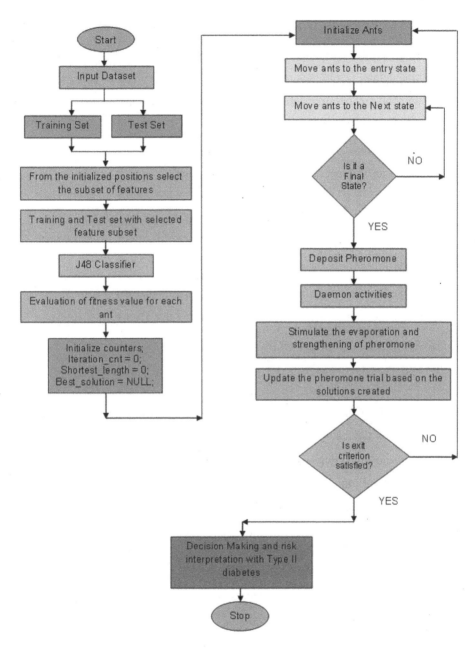

FIGURE 4.2 Proposed methodological workflow using ACO – decision trees.

Procedure 4.1 Procedure of proposed ACO – Decision tree model

Input:

Training dataset D with $m \times n$ matrix (n-dimensional)

m – the total number of training data features

C – the total number of iterations

A – the total ants in the group with the environment

F – the number of features selected upon execution

Output:

$\overline{D}$ – the total number of selected features at the final stage of execution

Algorithm:

01: **begin**

02: Frame the relevance matrix r_i for each feature such that $\forall\ i = 1 \ldots n$

03: Frame the similarity matrix $S_{i,j}$ for the feature set $\forall\ i, j = 1 \ldots n$

04: Assign heuristic value $\eta_1(F_i) = r_i, \eta_2(F_i, F_j) = \dfrac{1}{S_{i,j}}\ \forall i, j = 1 \ldots n$

05: Initialize pheromone values $\tau_i(1)$ which then associated with feature set $\forall\ i, j = 1 \ldots n$

06: **for** $p = 1$ to C **do**

07: Assign initial feature counter value $FC(i)$ to zero, $\forall\ i, j = 1 \ldots n$

08: Set the ants in a random fashion over the graphical nodes

09: **for** $i = 1$ to F **do**

10: **for** $k = 1$ to A **do**

11: select the subsequent unvisited feature f affording to the state transition rule

12: change the kth ant to newly selected feature f

13: increment the feature counter value allied with feature f

14: **end for**

15: **end for**

16: pheromone updating pertaining to the rule

17: **end for**

18: sort the features with descending order of value corresponding to τ_i

19: create $\overline{D}$ from D

20: **end**

Algorithm Decision Tree

01: **begin**

02: **for** $d = 1$ to number of training observations and its class values

03: **for** $a = 1$ to number of candidate attributes

04: Select a splitting criterion

05: **end for**

06: **end for**

07: Create a node N_d

08: **if** all observations in the training dataset have the same class output value C,

then

09: return N_d as a leaf node labeled with C

10: **if** attribute list $= \{\phi\}$, **then**

11: return N_d as a leaf node labeled with majority class output value.

12: Apply selected splitting criterion

13: Label node N_d with the splitting criterion attribute.

14: Remove the splitting criterion attribute from the attribute list

15: **for** each value i in the splitting criterion attribute

16: $D_i =$ no. of observations in training data satisfying attribute value i.

17: **if** D_i is empty then

18: attach a leaf node labeled with majority value to node N_d

19: **else**

20: attach the node returned by decision tree to node N_d

21: **end if**

22: **end for**

23: return node N_d

24: **end if**

25: **end if**

26: **for** $i = 1$ to number of training tuples (N)

27: **if** $\text{Class}_i = \text{Predicted Class}_i$ of testing data **then**

28: **if** Class$_i$ = Class label of positive tuples **then**

29: TP = TP + 1

30: **else if** Class$_i$ = Class label of negative tuples **then**

31:TN = TN + 1

32: **end if**

33: **end if**

34: **end for**

35: Fitness function $= (TP + TN/N)$

36: **end**

4.3 EXPERIMENTATION OF THE DEVELOPED MODEL OVER VARIOUS MEDICAL DATASETS

The experimentation has been made using both real-world and repository data. The repository data have been collected, pre-processed, and made ready for data processing upon model development. The following section illustrates the experimental results observed from type II diabetes, heart disease, cancer, and retinopathy datasets. The following are the metrics considered for evaluation in evaluating the collected data:

- Accuracy
- Error rate
- Kappa statistics
- Precision
- Recall
- Spearman's rho
- Root Mean Squared error
- Correlation

4.3.1 REAL-WORLD DATASETS

The real-world data corresponding to type II diabetes have been collected under the supervision of a medical expert over period of years. The collected data are formulated into a processable format of representation upon considering the necessary attributes for evaluation.

4.3.1.1 Type II Diabetes

The attributes include Age, Fasting blood glucose, Postprandial plasma glucose, A1c-Glycosylated Hemoglobin, Mean blood glucose, Total blood cholesterol, Blood Urea, Non-High-Density Lipoprotein cholesterol, Very-Low-Density Lipoprotein cholesterol, Tri-Glyceride Level, Low-Density Lipoprotein cholesterol, High-Density Lipoprotein cholesterol, Streptokinase, Albumin Creatinine Ratio, Total Protein,

Albumin, Globulin, Serum Glutamic Oxaloacetic Transaminase, Serum Glutamic Pyruvic Transaminase, Alkaline Phosphatase Test, Glutamyl transpeptidase, Hemo, and class label. Table 4.1 describes the results obtained with various performance metrics upon iterations.

With the entire set of iterations, the features selected are Fasting Plasma Glucose (FPG), Total Cholesterol, Blood Urea, Serum Glutamic Pyruvic Transaminase, Non-High-Density Lipoprotein cholesterol, Serum Glutamic Oxaloacetic Transaminase, Glutamyl transpeptidase, Albumin, Globulin, Total Protein, and High-Density Lipoprotein cholesterol.

4.3.1.2 Heart Disease

The interpretation of real-world heart disease dataset has been made with the proposed algorithmic model. The features selected at the final stage of iteration are age, chest pain type, systolic blood pressure, diastolic blood pressure, serum cholesterol, fasting blood sugar, restecg, waist circumference, smoking, hyper cholesterol, anterolateral, inferolateral, anteroseptal, septo anterior, obesity, and diabetes. The evaluation of the selected risk factors has been made with medical experts as a sort of external validation in order to determine the efficacy of the model. The experts revealed that some of the risk factors are reliable to be important, but some of the risk factors such as anterolateral, septo anterior, and age are found to be less important in nature. Moreover, the accuracy of the model with regard to heart disease dataset was found to be 42.51% which is not above the minimum scale of accuracy value which is about 50%. Table 4.2 describes the metrics observed from the real-world dataset. During the training and evaluation of heart disease dataset using ACO-DT algorithm, the movement of ants with regard to the pheromone values started initially with an accuracy value of 42.51%. Subsequently, it stagnated to an accuracy level of 39.88%, which is quite lesser than the previous level accuracy even if the features get reduced. This is mainly due to the stagnation of pheromone value of each attribute with its associated feature, which makes the subsequent iteration to have the same accuracy value.

4.3.2 Benchmark Datasets

The same process has been tested with benchmark dataset, such as Pima Indian diabetic data, cancer data which corresponds to benign and malignant cancer and Cleveland heart disease and Diabetic retinopathy dataset. Different values for the metrics have been observed with regard to the performance metrics. Tables 4.3–4.6 describe the parametric values observed for benchmark datasets.

With Pima Indian diabetic dataset, the features selected are pregnancy, glucose, blood pressure, thickness, insulin, weight, and pedigree function. Among eight features, seven have been selected by the algorithm which is being considered to be the worst-case scenario with feature selection process.

The attributes selected for Cleveland heart disease dataset correspond to age, chest pain type, trestbps, fasting blood sugar, restecg, exang, oldpeak, slope, and ca. Again, the number of features selected by the model is high when compared with the properties of feature selection techniques. Also, the features selected for cancer

TABLE 4.1

Results Obtained for Type II Diabetic Data with the Highest Level of Accuracy

Iterations	Accuracy	Error	Kappa	Recall	Precision	Rho	RMS Error	Correlation	Features Selected
Iteration 85	92.8	7.2	0.84	91.7	92.71	0.84	0.242	0.844	11
Iteration 86	91.6	8.4	0.82	90.9	91.26	0.82	0.261	0.821	16
Iteration 87	91.8	8.2	0.82	90.9	91.8	0.83	0.266	0.827	15
Iteration 88	89.2	10.8	0.76	86.7	90.23	0.77	0.3	0.768	13
Iteration 89	91.6	8.4	0.82	90.4	91.47	0.82	0.268	0.818	11
Iteration 90	92	8	0.83	91.4	91.69	0.83	0.255	0.831	17
Iteration 91	88	12	0.74	86.6	88.11	0.75	0.317	0.746	15
Iteration 92	89	11	0.76	87.2	88.97	0.76	0.303	0.761	14
Iteration 93	87.4	12.6	0.72	85.2	81.42	0.73	0.32	0.725	13
Iteration 94	94.6	5.4	0.88	93.9	94.5	0.89	0.207	0.884	11
Iteration 95	90.6	9.4	0.80	89.4	90.45	0.80	0.289	0.798	14
Iteration 96	83.6	16.4	0.62	79.6	84.67	0.6	0.368	0.64	15
Iteration 97	92.4	7.6	0.83	91.5	92.49	0.84	0.245	0.839	14
Iteration 98	91.8	8.2	0.82	90.7	91.75	0.82	0.254	0.824	15
Iteration 99	92.6	7.4	0.84	91.9	92.29	0.84	0.247	0.842	13
Iteration 100	91.8	8.2	0.87	89.6	92.83	0.82	0.269	0.823	15

TABLE 4.2

Results Obtained for Heart Disease Data with the Highest Level of Accuracy

Iteration	Accuracy	Error	Kappa	Recall	Precision	Rho	RMS Error	Correlation	Features Selected
Iteration 1	42.51	57.5	0.106	34.9	34.94	0.1	0.68	0.099	16
Iteration 2	39.22	60.8	0.048	32.1	32.6	0.06	0.702	0.057	14
Iteration 3	39.88	60.1	0.048	25	9.97	0.06	0.701	0.057	15
Iteration 4	39.88	60.1	0.048	25	9.97	0.06	0.701	0.057	17
Iteration 5	39.88	60.1	0.048	25	9.97	0.06	0.701	0.057	15
Iteration 6	39.88	60.1	0.048	25	9.97	0.06	0.701	0.057	15
Iteration 7	39.88	60.1	0.048	25	9.97	0.06	0.701	0.057	14
Iteration 8	39.88	60.1	0.048	25	9.97	0.06	0.701	0.057	15
Iteration 9	39.88	60.1	0.048	25	9.97	0.06	0.701	0.057	15
Iteration 10	39.88	60.1	0.048	25	9.97	0.06	0.701	0.057	15
Iteration 11	39.88	60.1	0.048	25	9.97	0.06	0.701	0.057	14
Iteration 12	39.88	60.1	0.048	25	9.97	0.06	0.701	0.057	15
Iteration 13	39.88	60.1	0.048	25	9.97	0.06	0.701	0.057	14
Iteration 14	39.88	60.1	0.048	25	9.97	0.06	0.701	0.057	13
Iteration 15	39.88	60.1	0.048	25	9.97	0.06	0.701	0.057	14
Iteration 16	39.88	60.1	0.048	25	9.97	0.06	0.701	0.057	15

TABLE 4.3

Results Obtained for Pima Indian Diabetic Data with the Highest Level of Accuracy

Iteration	Accuracy	Error	Kappa	Recall	Precision	Rho	RMS Error	Correlation	Features Selected
Iteration 1	70.32	29.7	0.28	64.1	64.48	0.298	0.464	0.298	5
Iteration 2	72.58	27.4	0.31	64.0	72.9	0.349	0.453	0.349	6
Iteration 3	65.99	34.0	0.03	51.8	44.09	0.032	0.408	0.032	5
Iteration 4	73.86	26.1	0.31	63.6	77.51	0.378	0.443	0.378	7
Iteration 5	73.86	26.1	0.34	65.4	75.55	0.385	0.444	0.385	7
Iteration 6	72.59	27.4	0.29	63	73.67	0.342	0.447	0.342	5
Iteration 7	72.57	27.4	0.3	63.8	73.49	0.346	0.45	0.346	6
Iteration 8	71.08	28.9	0.30	65.1	65.43	0.317	0.458	0.317	4
Iteration 9	73.86	26.1	0.31	63.6	77.51	0.378	0.443	0.378	7
Iteration 10	72.58	27.4	0.29	63.2	73.86	0.345	0.454	0.345	5
Iteration 11	72.33	27.7	0.30	64.2	72.1	0.344	0.448	0.344	5
Iteration 12	72.58	27.4	0.29	62.9	75.33	0.349	0.447	0.349	5
Iteration 13	72.85	27.2	0.30	63.8	74.02	0.354	0.452	0.354	6
Iteration 14	72.33	27.7	0.30	63.8	71.95	0.339	0.457	0.339	6

TABLE 4.4

Results Obtained for Cleveland Heart Disease Dataset with the Highest Level of Accuracy

Iteration	Accuracy	Error	Kappa	Recall	Precision	Rho	RMS Error	Correlation	Features Selected
Iteration 1	73.7	26.3	0.454	72.17	75.27	0.473	0.464	0.473	8
Iteration 2	77.78	22.22	0.544	76.83	79.25	0.56	0.423	0.56	7
Iteration 3	77.41	22.59	0.537	76.58	78.64	0.551	0.434	0.551	10
Iteration 4	73.7	26.3	0.458	72.33	75.55	0.477	0.437	0.477	7
Iteration 5	73.7	26.3	0.459	72.58	74.69	0.472	0.465	0.472	9
Iteration 6	70.37	29.63	0.396	69.75	70.98	0.406	0.483	0.406	6
Iteration 7	74.44	25.56	0.474	73.33	75.86	0.491	0.458	0.491	8
Iteration 8	70	30	0.388	69.33	70.6	0.398	0.488	0.398	8
Iteration 9	77.04	22.96	0.531	76.33	78.03	0.543	0.418	0.543	7
Iteration 10	74.44	25.56	0.476	73.5	75.04	0.485	0.448	0.485	8
Iteration 11	76.67	23.33	0.519	75.5	78.1	0.535	0.425	0.535	6
Iteration 12	79.63	20.37	0.584	78.92	80.29	0.592	0.407	0.592	9

TABLE 4.5
Results Obtained for Cancer Dataset with the Highest Level of Accuracy

Iteration	Accuracy	Error	Kappa	Recall	Precision	Rho	RMS Error	Correlation	Features Selected
Iteration 1	94.42	5.58	0.878	94.38	93.8	0.882	0.218	0.882	5
Iteration 2	94.71	5.29	0.884	94.58	94	0.886	0.202	0.886	8
Iteration 3	94.57	5.43	0.881	94.5	93.93	0.884	0.205	0.884	6
Iteration 4	93.85	6.15	0.865	93.65	93.3	0.869	0.266	0.869	8
Iteration 5	93.42	6.58	0.857	93.21	92.85	0.86	0.229	0.86	5
Iteration 6	94.42	5.58	0.876	93.49	94.46	0.879	0.219	0.879	4
Iteration 7	94.57	5.43	0.882	94.5	93.91	0.884	0.206	0.884	6
Iteration 8	94.71	5.29	0.885	94.6	94.2	0.888	0.214	0.888	9
Iteration 9	94.99	5.01	0.89	94.81	94.52	0.893	0.207	0.893	7

TABLE 4.6
Results Obtained for Diabetic Retinopathy Dataset with the Highest Level of Accuracy

Iteration	Accuracy	Error	Kappa	Recall	Precision	Rho	RMS Error	Correlation	Features Selected
Iteration 1	53.78	46.22	0.027	51.31	57.01	0.075	0.487	0.075	13
Iteration 2	53.08	46.92	0.022	51.17	48.44	0.047	0.49	0.047	13
Iteration 3	53.61	46.39	0.014	50.64	52.54	0.04	0.492	0.04	11
Iteration 4	53.17	46.83	0.07	53.64	64.23	0.139	0.487	0.139	12
Iteration 5	53.43	46.57	0.031	51.55	57.29	0.079	0.489	0.079	13
Iteration 6	53.52	46.48	0.021	51.07	47.7	0.048	0.49	0.048	13
Iteration 7	53.87	46.13	0.029	51.45	55.44	0.07	0.49	0.07	14
Iteration 8	53	47	0.043	52.2	57.25	0.089	0.489	0.089	12
Iteration 9	53.96	46.04	0.072	53.69	64.95	0.143	0.49	0.143	13
Iteration 10	54.21	45.79	0.046	52.36	62.11	0.096	0.492	0.096	15
Iteration 11	53.43	46.57	0.049	52.56	57.67	0.098	0.493	0.098	15
Iteration 12	52.91	47.09	0.019	51.01	51.71	0.045	0.491	0.045	9
Iteration 13	53.69	46.31	0.016	50.73	58.82	0.052	0.493	0.052	10
Iteration 14	53.35	46.65	0.009	50.41	49.15	0.016	0.495	0.016	13
Iteration 15	53.52	46.48	0.067	53.51	65.46	0.138	0.487	0.138	11

TABLE 4.7

Summary of Accuracy Values and Features Selected with the Proposed Approach

S.No.	Dataset	Total Records	Total Number of Attributes	Accuracy	Number of Features Selected
1	Type II diabetic	762	22	94.6	11
2	Heart disease	306	24	42.51	16
3	Pima Indian diabetes	394	8	73.86	7
4	Cleveland heart disease	270	13	79.63	9
5	Cancer	699	9	94.99	7
6	Diabetic retinopathy	1,151	19	54.21	15

dataset include normal nucleoli, uniformity in cell size, shape, nuclei, epithelial cell size, mitoses, and thickness. Similarly, for diabetic retinopathy dataset, the features selected are binary result in quality assessment, and the result in detection exudates information, distance measure, and binary measurement. Table 4.7 summarizes the maximum accuracy obtained with regard to the total number of features selected for the datasets considered.

With the proposed approach for feature selection and classification using ACO – decision trees, the accuracy level for some of the datasets has been found to be below the average level of 50%. In addition to this, the total number of features selected by the model isn't found to be minimal with regard to the principles of feature selection mechanism. Hence, this model isn't found to be acceptable for medical data analysis with regard to feature selection and classification process. Even with some of the datasets, the accuracy was found to be greater than 90%, but the number of features is found to be the same as that of the original dataset. Therefore, more forms of parametric evaluation have to be made with regard to ACO for implementing medical data.

4.4 ANALYSIS OF TIME COMPLEXITY

Consider f is the number of features and n is the number of patterns generated, and then the relevance matrix is executed and evaluated using the term variance matrix. Therefore, the complexity is $O(fn)$. In addition to this, the similarity measures are computed for each set of feature pair upon iterations. Then, the time complexity is represented as $O(f^2n)$. Therefore, the total time complexity is $O(fn + f^2n) = O(f^2n)$. Moreover, the ants explore the search space in a different perspective over iterations C. Hence, the time complexity with regard to this measure is given as $O(CAFf)$, where F corresponds to the total number of features selected by each of the ants during each iteration. During the next step of the algorithm, the pheromone values are sorted with time measure of about $O(n \log n)$. Hence, total time complexity is illustrated in the following equation:

$$O\left(n^2 p + CFn + n\log n\right) = O\left(n^2 p + CFn\right) \qquad (4.5)$$

In general, $F \ll n$.

Therefore, the measure of time complexity is given in the following equation:

$$O\left(n^2 p\right) \qquad (4.6)$$

Hence, the proposed method provides an iterative improvement when related to that of existing filter methods. Therefore, the time complexity of the proposed method is little more expensive than that of the existing methods in practice.

4.5 DETERMINATION OF RISK CORRELATION WITH SELECTED FEATURES

The number of features selected by the proposed approach is more when compared to the existing approaches. Also, the accuracy corresponding to some of the dataset is not acceptable to an average nominal value of about 50%. So, with the set of features selected, there are some of the irrelevant features that don't provide any importance to the disease specified. Therefore, as a concluding remark, the correlation among the risk factors doesn't convey the predominance among the risk with regard to the risk factors among the real-world data in terms of locality and the likelihood of people.

4.6 SUMMARY

This chapter deals with the proposed mechanism of ACO – decision tree for predicting the risk related to medical data. More specifically, two different real-world data have been used to identify the most predominant risk factors that contribute toward the disease. The proposed module includes the process of pheromone initialization, feature selection based on state transition rule, updating of pheromone values, using update rule, and building the feature set with top pheromone values. The fitness function is then evaluated using Java execution of C4.5 decision tree algorithm. The experimental results show that feature selection using ACO – decision trees doesn't provide minimal number of relevant features with maximum classification accuracy. The evaluation has also been made with benchmark datasets for diseases such as Pima Indian diabetes, heart disease, cancer, and diabetic retinopathy. The results showed the maximum accuracy value of about 94.99% for cancer dataset by selecting seven features among the total of nine features. Also, for real-world dataset, the maximum accuracy has been observed for type II diabetic dataset with 94.6% by selecting 11 out of a total of 22 features.

Hence, there is a need for an improved algorithmic model for predicting the risk that resembles the disease across a specific region. The algorithmic model must also have the ability to determine the minimum number of relevant and dependent features with improved accuracy.

REFERENCES

1. Anne Szczepańska. (2011). Research Design and Statistical Analysis, Third Edition by Jerome L. Myers, Arnold D. Well, Robert F. Lorch, Jr. *International Statistical Review* [Internet]. 2011 Nov 21; 79(3), 491–492. doi:10.1111/j.1751-5823.2011.00159_12.x

2. Xie Jiachen, Li Xinming, Li Yib. (2012). Research on DDoS Defense Technology Based on Ant Colony Optimization. *Computer Engineering*, 38(17), 145–147.

3. Alberto Colorni, Marco Dorigo, Vittorio Maniezzo, Reinhard Männer, Bernard Manderick. (1992). An Investigation of Some Properties of an Ant Algorithm. *Parallel Problem Solving from Nature 2, PPSN-II*, Brussels, Belgium, September 28–30, 1992, 515–526.

4. Robert Gentleman, Vincent J. Carey, Douglas M. Bates, Benjamin M. Bolstad, Marcel Dettling, Sandrine Dudoit, Byron Ellis, Laurent Gautier, Yongchao Ge, Jeff Gentry, Kurt Hornik, Torsten Hothorn, Wolfgang Huber, Stefano Maria Iacus, Rafael A. Irizarry, Friedrich Leisch, Cheng Li, Martin Maechler, A. J. Rossini, Günther Sawitzki, Colin A. Smith, Gordon K. Smyth, Luke Tierney, Jean Yang, Jianhua Zhang. (2004). Bioconductor: Open Software Development for Computational Biology and Bioinformatics. *Genome Biology*, 5(10), 1–16. doi:10.1186/GB-2004-5-10-R80

5. Rafael Stubs Parpinelli, Heitor Silvério Lopes, Alex A. Freitas. (2002). Data Mining with an Ant Colony Optimization Algorithm. *IEEE Transactions on Evolutionary Computation*, 6(4), 321–332. doi:10.1109/TEVC.2002.802452

6. Shin, Ando., H., Iba. (2002). Ant Algorithm for Construction of Evolutionary Tree. *Proceedings of the 2002 Congress on Evolutionary Computation*, 2, 1552–1557. doi:10.1109/CEC.2002.1004473

7. El-Ghazali Talbi, Olivier Roux, Cyril Fonlupt, D. Robillard. (2001). Parallel Ant Colonies for the Quadratic Assignment Problem. *Future Generation Computer Systems*, 17(4), 441–449. doi:10.1016/S0167-739X(99)00124-7

8. Gerardo Beni, Jing Wang. (1993). Swarm Intelligence in Cellular Robotic Systems. *Robots and Biological Systems: Towards a New Bionics*, 703–712. doi:10.1007/978-3-642-58069-7_38

9. Alberto Colorni, Marco Dorigo, Vittorio Maniezzo, Marco Trubian. (1994). Ant System for Job-Shop Scheduling. *Statistics and Computer Science*, 34(1), 39–53.

10. Kwang Y. Lee, J. G. Vlachogiannis. (2005). Optimization of Power Systems based on Ant Colony System Algorithms: An Overview. *Proceedings of the 13th International Conference on, Intelligent Systems Application to Power Systems*, Arlington, VA, USA, 22–35. doi:10.1109/ISAP.2005.1599237

11. Yanjun, Li, Tie-Jun, Wu. (2002). A Nested Ant Colony Algorithm for Hybrid Production Scheduling. *Proceedings of the American Control Conference*, 2(1), 1123–1128. doi:10.1109/ACC.2002.1023170

12. Walter J. Gutjahr. (2000). A Graph-Based Ant System and Its Convergence. *Future Generation Computer Systems*, 16(9), 873–888. doi:10.1016/S0167-739X(00)00044-3

13. Luca Maria Gambardella, Marco Dorigo. (1995). Ant-Q: A Reinforcement Learning Approach to the Traveling Salesman Problem. *Machine Learning, Proceedings of the Twelfth International Conference on Machine Learning*, Tahoe City, California, USA, July 9-12, 252–260.

14. Israel A. Wagner, Michael Lindenbaum, Alfred M. Bruckstein. (1999). Distributed Covering by Ant-Robots Using Evaporating Traces. *IEEE Transactions on Robotics and Automation*, 15(5), 918–933. doi:10.1109/70.795795

15. Michael J. B. Krieger, Jean-Bernard Billeter, Laurent Keller. (2000). Ant-Like Task Allocation and Recruitment in Cooperative Robots. *Nature*, 406(6799), 992–995. doi:10.1038/35023164

16. Chao-Hsien Chu, Jun-Hua Gu, Xiang Dan Hou, Qijun Gu. (2002). A Heuristic Ant Algorithm for Solving QoS Multicast Routing Problem. *Proceedings of the 2002 Congress on Evolutionary Computation*, 2, 1630–1635. doi:10.1109/CEC.2002.1004486

17. M. Stone. (1974). Cross-Validatory Choice and Assessment of Statistical Predictions. *Journal of the Royal Statistical Society Series B-Methodological*, 36(2), 111–133. doi:10.1111/J.2517-6161.1974.TB00994.X

18. Ron Kohavi. (1995). A Study of Cross-Validation and Bootstrap for Accuracy Estimation and Model Selection. *International Joint Conferences on Artificial Intelligence*, 2, 1137–1143.

5 Predictive Analytics Using Bee-Based Harmony Search with Decision Trees for Medical Data

5.1 A REVIEW ON CLINICAL DATA ANALYSIS

Medical informatics focuses upon the use of computer knowledge to various fields in medicine such as healthcare, medical research, and discerning medical learning. It solves various problems related to health environment as well as provides value-based health information to arrive at a decision. Computer-aided exemplifications and methods provide computerized decision analysis for recommending ideal action in association with the record concerned with each patient [1]. The Australian center for behavioral research in diabetes provided a study and clinical traits with regard to diabetes (type II) [2]. The study protocol was published in Family Practice. The work provides a diabetic study and the probable risk factors corresponding to eye health with effective communications and intentions to eye screening [3]. The major risk corresponds to the Postprandial Plasma Glucose levels in blood with the moderate age groups [2].

The Diabetes of the United Kingdom Organization provided the remedial measures and the long-term effects to glucose levels, which turn out to the control over heart attacks. It also exemplifies the risk factors and measures that have been studied over the people and the treatments carried out in the region of United Kingdom.

The Indian diabetic research foundation has taken up a project for strengthening the national diabetic care services. The main intention of the project is to support the diabetic service and to create awareness among the people to be more explored with the risk factors, expenditures incurred, and its cause with regard to the region of the people, their dietary habits, and locality [4].

The primary goal of data mining and swarm intelligence techniques is to identify the valid, useful, and ultimately understandable patterns that exist among the data. It performs a useful inference from the data using the patterns learned [5]. The data mining computational methods provide the detection of event from high-dimensional healthcare records of any sort of disease and pave the way for detection and investigation.

DOI: 10.1201/9781003330189-5

Data analysis in healthcare is an exploring research area for building real-world decision support system. Identifying the healthcare problem and resolving its inconsistencies is a big problem. Mining healthcare data and providing a predictive model for specific diseases is the one that is most extensively needed by healthcare experts.

5.2 DATA COLLECTION AND PRE-PROCESSING

Data from 732 consecutive diabetic cases were collected between the years 2012 and 2015 accordingly under a medical expert supervision. The dataset has been cleaned and processed, after which it should be ready for evaluation. Since the dataset comprises numerical values relative to each of the attribute, the values of the attributes range from a minimum to a maximum range. To make the dataset into an appropriate form for the mining process, the attribute values have to be scaled to fall within a small specified range. So, for this process, Z-Score normalization has been used. The following equation explains the method of Z-Score normalization:

$$X_{new} = \frac{(X_{old} - A_{mean})}{\sigma_A} \qquad (5.1)$$

where X_{new} is the new normalized value for a tuple of record corresponding to the variable A, X_{old} is the existing value for a tuple of record corresponding to the variable A, A_{mean} is the mean value of the attribute A, and σ_A is the standard deviation of the attribute A.

From the set of records, the optimized feature set is identified by applying Bee-based Harmony Search (BHS) algorithm and decision tree algorithm with a linear mathematical model. Finally, for each set of records and their corresponding class labels with its optimized set of features, it is analyzed and evaluated by medical experts. The developed predictive model can be effectively utilized for the existence of the type of diabetes by medical professionals for its evaluation. To evaluate the dataset, the values with the corresponding attribute have been classified into various levels as given in Table 5.1.

The A1c levels can be compared with respect to that of the mean blood glucose tolerance level. The value of A1c conveys an average level of blood sugar control for the past 3 months, and hence, the control level is managed with home monitoring system for alteration toward medications in diabetes. Table 5.2 illustrates the A1c levels to that of the mean blood glucose level [6].

Similarly, consecutive CHD subjects of about 306 records have been collected from a hospital under the supervision of a medical expert. The dataset consists of about 24 attributes, with class labels of four categories corresponding to the stages of heart disease.

The attributes are of type categorical and continuous in accordance with the data values. If the data type is categorical, we need to check its consistency over nominal-, ordinal-, and binary-valued representation. The continuous valued attributes should be checked with respect to the range of values. In order to make the continuous data values into smaller specified range, Min-Max normalization has been used. This can be computed using the following equation:

TABLE 5.1
Leveling of Attributes

S.No.	Attributes	Level 1	Level 2	Level 3	Level 4
1	Age	≤20	>20 to ≤30	>30 to ≤50	>50
2	Fasting Plasma Glucose (FPG)	70 and 99 mg/dL	above 99 mg/dL	-	-
3	Postprandial plasma Glucose (PPG)	Normal: below 7.8 mmol/L (140 mg/dL)	Impaired glucose tolerance:7.8 and 11.1 mmol/L (140 and 200 mg/dL)	Diabetes: equal or above 11.1 mmol/L (200 mg/dL)	-
4	Glycosylated Hemoglobin (A1c)	Normal: between 4% and 5.6%	Increased Risk: between 5.7% and 6.4%	Levels of 6.5% or higher indicate value of diabetes	-
5	Mean Blood Glucose (MBG)	Normal: around 90–130 mg/dL)	-	-	-
6	Total blood cholesterol	Normal: 200 mg/dL (5.2 mmol/L)	Risk: 200–239 mg/dL (5.2 and 6.2 mmol/L)	High Risk: 240 and above (6.3 mmol/L)	-
7	Blood Urea	Normal: 13–43 mg/dL	Risk: 43–55 mg/dL	High Risk: 55 and above mg/dL	-
8	Non-High-Density Lipoprotein cholesterol	Near Ideal value: 130–159 mg/dL (3.4–4.0 mmol/L)	Borderline value High: 160–189 mg/dL (4.1–4.8 mmol/L)	Higher: 190–219 mg/dL (4.9–5.6 mmol/L)	Very High: greater than 220 mg/dL (5.7 mmol/L)
9	Very-Low-Density Lipoprotein cholesterol	Optimum: <20 mg/dL	Risk: >30 mg/dL	Serious risk: >40 mL/dL	
10	Tri-Glyceride Level (TGL)	Optimal level 150 mg/dL	Risk 150–199 mg/dL	Risk 200–499 mg/dL	Above 500 elevated risk
11	Low-Density Lipoprotein (LDL) cholesterol	Normal <100 mg/dL	Between 100 and 129 mg/dL ideal	Risk 130–159 mg/dL is elevated	Above 190 elevated risk
12	High-Density Lipoprotein (HDL) cholesterol	Normal 40 mg/dL for men and 50 mg/dL for women	Between 40–49 mg/dL and 50–59 mg/dL ideal	Above 60 mg/dL is at risk	

(*Continued*)

TABLE 5.1 (*Continued*)
Leveling of Attributes

S.No.	Attributes	Level 1	Level 2	Level 3	Level 4
13	Streptokinase (SK)	Infuse 45 mL within 60 min	Infusion 3 mL/h		
14	Albumin Creatinine Ratio (ACR)	Normal: <2.0 for men and <2.8 for women	Above 2.0 and 2.8 at risk		
15	Total Protein	Normal: 6 and 8.3 g/dL	Above 8.3 at risk		
16	Albumin	Normal: 3.4–5.4 g/dL	Above 5.4 g/dL at risk		
17	Globulin	Normal: 2.0–3.5 g/dL	Above 3.5 g/dL at risk		
18	Serum Glutamic Oxaloacetic Transaminase (SGOT)	Normal 8–40 U/L in male and 6–34 in female	Above 40 and 34 at risk		
19	Serum Glutamic-Pyruvic Transaminase (SGPT)	Normal <34 in Male and <52 in females	Above 34 and 52 at risk		
20	Alkaline Phosphatase Test (ALP)	Normal: 44–147 U/L	Above 147 at Risk		
21	Glutamyl trans-peptidase (GGT)	Normal: 8–65 U/L	Above 65 at Risk		
22	Hemo (HB)	12.1–15.1 g/dL for females 13.6–17.7 g/dL in males			

TABLE 5.2
Estimated A1c Level with Average Blood Glucose

A1c Level (%)	Average Blood Glucose (mg/dL)	A1c Level (%)	Average Blood Glucose (mg/dL)
14	335	9	212
13	326	8	183
12	298	7	154
11	269	6	126
10	240	5	97

$$v' = \frac{v - \text{Min}_A}{\text{Max}_A - \text{Min}_A}\left(\text{new}_{\text{Max}_A} - \text{new}_{\text{min}\_A}\right) + \text{new}_{\text{min}\_A} \qquad (5.2)$$

where Min_A is the minimum value over all the records corresponding to the attribute, Max_A is the maximum value over all the records corresponding to the attribute, $\text{new}_{\text{min}\_A}$ is the newly adopted minimum value for the attribute (0), and $\text{new}_{\text{max}\_A}$ is the newly adopted maximum value for the attribute (1).

While considering the real data which have been collected from the regional hospital containing 25 attributes including the class label (from Table 5.1), it has to be observed that the attribute Smoking to Pericardial effusion is of type binary since it signifies the presence or absence of the syndrome. The attribute Chest pain type has various differentiation based upon the disease condition and it is categorized as nominal-valued attribute. The other attributes are normalized using min-max normalization.

5.3 PATHOGENESIS OF NON-COMMUNICABLE DISEASES

According to the World Health Organization (WHO), diabetes is one of the major health problems in most of the countries. It concerns to the improper regulation of insulin level in the human body, which may lead to other NCD [7]. For the year 2014, it is found that the global prevalence is estimated to be 9% among adults with the age of 18+ years [8]. During 2012, it was found that 1.5 million deaths were directly caused due to diabetes [9]. The WHO suggests that diabetes will be the seventh leading cause of death by 2030 [10].

Similarly, heart disease is also one of the most predominant diseases in India. Heart disease is caused due to the contraction of blood vessels which supply oxygen-rich blood to the heart. Therefore, it is the result of atherosclerosis. Plaque (cholesterol constituents) accumulates over the walls of the arteries. This causes insufficient supply of oxygen carrying blood to the heart.

Among the 57 million deaths during 2008, 36 million were due to Non-Communicable Diseases. The major Non-Communicable Disease deaths in 2008 correspond to cardiac disease. Cardiovascular diseases are considered to be the major cause of death and infirmity in India by 2020, as per WHO report. By 2030, it is expected that 23 million people will die from CHDs annually. Therefore, effective preventive measures should be taken to prevent 'life threatening' diseases such as heart disease.

Recent advances in medical technology generate large amounts of different categories of data. The identified dataset may be categorical or in the continuous form. Some data such as temperature, age, cholesterol level, and blood sugar level may be in the form of images, echo-cardiogram signals, and/or continuous values representation [11]. The phenomenon of extracting useful data and providing a proper form of decision analysis process for the effective diagnosis and treatment toward a specific disease becomes important [12].

Developments in the field of clinical research have been carried out to identify the risk factors related to NCD. However, this has not reduced the impact and the spread of the disease. There exist various factors that subsidize toward the expansion of NCD, which can have modifiable and non-modifiable risk factors. Therapeutic procedures are also termed as the medical procedure that is a line of action mainly anticipated to attain a result in caring for a person with health problems. The measurement of the patient's condition is made with respect to the medical test. Each disease corresponds to various parameters that signify the presence of the disease. The values of the parameters determine whether a patient has the disease or not. In accordance with NCD, the probable procedures are blood level monitoring, obesity management, non-acute medical condition (family history, leanness), insulin therapy, glucose level management, and HDL cholesterol levels management.

5.4 PROPOSED MODEL USING BHS – DECISION TREES

5.4.1 HARMONY MEMORY INITIALIZATION

Harmony Search is a meta-heuristic algorithm inspired by the improvisation of musicians. Each musician plays a note in finding a best harmony solution all together. In other words, each decision variable generates a value in finding a global optimum. Harmony Search works relatively toward the improvement of the variable selection strategy to attain a set of optimized features. If the optimized set of features doesn't satisfy the condition of fitness evaluation, then the features are improvised to attain the target level. The process of improvisation delivers a good way for feature selection in Harmony Search algorithm. Meanwhile, it should adhere to any of the following rules [13]:

1. Selecting any value from the memory of Harmony Search
2. Selecting an adjacent value
3. Selecting a random value from the given specified range

The above rules strictly depend on and adhere to the state of the Harmony Memory Consideration Rate (HMCR) and Pitch Adjusting Rate (PAR) for the feature that has to be selected. The HMCR and PAR have control over the result and with a convergence speed. To start up with the process, the Harmony Memory needs to be initialized. The memory signifies randomly generated results for the problem considered under optimization. When considering an n-dimensional problem, the memory state is represented in the following equation:

$$x[i,1], x[i,2], x[i,n] \tag{5.3}$$

Similar to the above matrix row, the corresponding rows get formulated up to the HMCR value. The value of i ranges from $i = 1, 2, 3, \ldots$ HMS, which is a typical solution. The next step is to create a new solution as in the following equation:

$$\left[x_1', x_2', x_3' \ldots x_n'\right] \tag{5.4}$$

From the determined value of the Harmony Memory (HM), each of the specified compliments is obtained from the value of HMCR. Hence, it is defined as the maximum probability of selecting the HM members. Once this is over, HM is updated. Then, the new results for the matrix values get generated. As a result, it will replace the values. Otherwise, it gets eliminated. The above steps are repeated till the stopping criterion is reached. It can be set by the total number of iterations or the target fitness value. Harmony Search is a random search technique which won't require any prior knowledge of evaluation such as gradient descent and gradient functions. Hence, it only requires a single memory search criterion to evolve. The step-wise process is given as follows:

1. Initialize the variables and its parametric values.
2. Initialize the Harmony Memory.
3. Improvise with the new harmony value.
4. Update the Memory value concerning the Harmony Search.
5. Redo steps 2–4 till the ending stage is met.

5.4.2 MEMORY CONCERN IN HARMONY SEARCH

The BHS algorithm modifies the memory consideration rule of the Harmony Search. In Harmony Search, the exploitation is mainly controlled by HMCR value [14]. A high HMCR value indicates that the good solution from the historical Harmony Memory is likely to be selected. This gives rise to a lower rate of convergence, which is suitable for the search process to be optimized. To overcome this, a mutation process involved in the Artificial Bee Colony Optimization method is employed in the Harmony Search algorithm. In BHS-J48, the feature selection is carried out using the BHS algorithm, and the fitness is evaluated for each selected feature by J48 classifier. Figure 5.1 depicts the methodological workflow of the proposed BHS decision tree algorithm.

5.4.3 CLASSIFICATION OVER SELECTED FEATURES USING DECISION TREES

Once the feature set is extracted, it is fed up to the C4.5 algorithm which is also termed as J48 (Java Execution of C4.5 Decision Tree algorithm). Decision trees are said to be one of the most efficient and scalable algorithms to map data observations about an item to derive conclusions corresponding to the items target value. A decision tree is used to build classification model in the form of a tree-like structure based on certain condition with class-labeled training tuples. The algorithm breaks down the whole dataset into smaller chunks from the root node until the designated leaf node is reached. Each of the internal nodes signifies a test on the attribute and each leaf node signifies the outcome of the test. The selection of the root node is based upon the chosen attribute selection measure. The attribute selection measure may be information gain, gain ratio, or Gini index. In accordance with the evaluation of the selected attributes, the tree uses one of the splitting measures to classify the class-labeled training tuples.

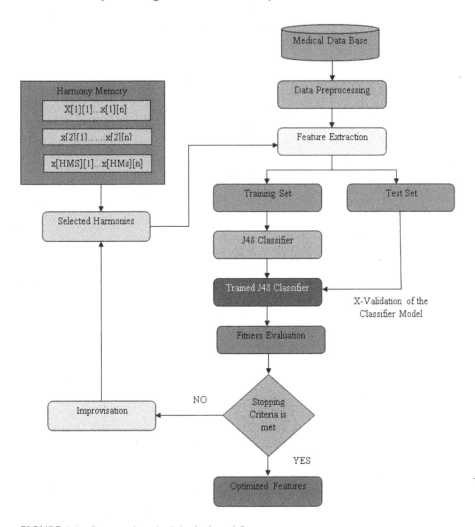

FIGURE 5.1   Proposed methodological workflow.

5.4.4 SELECTION OF SPLITTING CRITERION

The execution of the decision tree depends on the splitting criterion, which specifies how the split has to be made in accordance with the input attributes and the class label. The splitting criterion can be fixed based on the performance of the decision tree algorithm for the observed data. The following splitting measures have been investigated for our problem with brief representation [15]:

  1. Information gain:
        The indication to classify a tuple over D is expressed in the following equation:

$$\text{Info}(D) = -\sum_{i-1}^{m} p_i \log_2(p_i) \tag{5.5}$$

If we have to partition the data tuples in D on the given attribute A having v distinct values, $\{a_1, a_2, a_3, \ldots a_v\}$ as observed from the training data, then the information needed after partitioning is measured by the following equation:

$$\text{Info}(D) = \sum_{j-1}^{v} \frac{|D_j|}{|D|}(D_j) \tag{5.6}$$

2. Gain ratio:

Gain ratio estimates info (D) with split info significance which derived over standardizing the value of info gain. The info (D) is expressed in the following equation:

$$\text{Split Info}_A(D) = -\sum_{j-1}^{v} \frac{|D_j|}{|D|} \times \log_2 \left(\frac{|D_j|}{|D|} \right) \tag{5.7}$$

The gain ratio is defined in the following equation:

$$\text{Gain Ratio}(A) = \frac{\text{Gain}(A)}{\text{Split Info}(A)} \tag{5.8}$$

3. Gini index:

The impurity over D is processed through Gini index in the following equations:

$$\text{Gini}(D) = 1 - \sum_{i-1}^{m} p_i^2 \tag{5.9}$$

$$\text{Gini}_A(D) = -\frac{|D_1|}{|D|}\text{Gini}(D_1) + \frac{|D_2|}{|D|}\text{Gini}(D_2) \tag{5.10}$$

Information gain is probably a good measure, but it is not suitable for the attributes having a larger number of distinct values. Gini index, which is an impurity measure-based criterion, is suitable for the process of divergence between the target attribute values. It signifies the maximum probability distribution with the target attribute values. Therefore, the attribute selection measure gain ratio is used up for generating the decision tree for data classification. The BHS workflow is shown in Procedure 5.1.

Procedure 5.1 Proposed BHS algorithm

01: begin

02: Initialize Harmony memory size HMS = 10, HMCR = 0.9 No. of features (n)

03: Initialize the Harmony memory with random solutions X_a

04: **while**(fitness value<expected accuracy)

05: Evaluate the fitness by J48

06: **for** $i = 1$ to n

07: **if** $(\text{rand} < \text{HMCR})$

08: Identify the feature combinations

09: Perform fitness evaluation for each combination

10: Identify the best and worst harmony

11: The memory consideration for the next iteration is computed as,

12: $X_{\text{new}}(i) = X_a(i) + \varphi_a(i)(X_a(i) - X_k(i))$

13: Evaluate fitness for X_{new}

14: **if** $fit(X_{\text{new}}) > fit(X_a)$ then

15: Replace X_a with X_{new}

16: **end if**

17: **if** $(\text{randPAR} > \text{PAR})$

18: $X_{new}(i) = X_a + / - \text{rand}(\ ) * \text{BW}$

19: **end if**

20: **else**

21: Generate the New Harmony memory via randomization

22: **end if**

23: Accept the New Harmony solution (if better)

24: Update the harmony memory

25: **Next**

26: **end for**

27: **end while**

28: Find the best solution

29: **end**

In the BHS workflow, n denotes the number of attributes in the dataset. The modification for memory consideration is described as follows:

$$X_{new}(i) = X_a(i) + \varphi_a(i)\big(X_a(i) - X_k(i)\big) \tag{5.11}$$

where $X_{new}(i)$ is the new harmony for the ith decision variable with $a, k \in (1, 2, 3, 4, \ldots HMS)$ and $a \neq k$; $\varphi_a(i)$ is a random number between $(-1, 1)$.

The workflow of the proposed J48 workflow is given in Procedure 5.2.

Procedure 5.2 Workflow of J48 algorithm

01: begin

02: **for** $d = 1$ to number of training observations and its class values

03: **for** $a = 1$ to number of candidate attributes

04: Select a splitting criterion

05: **end for**

06: **end for**

07: Create a node N_d

08: **if** all observations in the training dataset have the same class output value C,

then

09: return N_d as a leaf node labeled with C

10: **if** attribute list $= \{\varphi\}$, **then**

11: return N_d as a leaf node labeled with majority class output value.

12: Apply selected splitting criterion

13: Label node N_d with the splitting criterion attribute.

14: Remove the splitting criterion attribute from the attribute list

15: **for** each value i in the splitting criterion attribute

16: $D_i =$ no. of observations in training data satisfying attribute value i.

17: **if** D_i is empty then

18: attach a leaf node labeled with majority value to node N_d

19: **else**

20: attach the node returned by decision tree to node N_d

21: **end if**

22: **end for**

23: return node N_d

24: **end if**

25: **end if**

26: **for** $i = 1$ to number of training tuples (N)

27: **if** $Class_i$ = Predicted $Class_i$ of testing data **then**

28: **if** $Class_i$ = Class label of positive tuples **then**

29: TP = TP + 1

30: **else if** $Class_i$ = Class label of negative tuples **then**

31: TN = TN + 1

32: **end if**

33: **end if**

34: **end for**

35: Fitness function = (TP + TN/N)

36: end

5.5 EXPERIMENTATION OF THE OBSERVED MODEL OVER VARIOUS MEDICAL DATASETS

5.5.1 PERFORMANCE METRICS

The performance of the Prediction Model is measured using the following metrics: The accuracy level as depicted in equation (5.12) conveys the performance of the model with regard to type II diabetic prediction for the given test case. During the analysis of accuracy in developing a predictive model, it has always been observed that the model provides the observed target value for a new set of data. The target of the accurate solution is always achieved by the training the model or the classifier of the system. The association between how well the model predicts on a new set of data and the training data can be expressed as sum of the training error and optimism results. The nature of the value of optimism determines how well the designed model behaves inferior for the new data when compared to the training data. The exact level of predicted accuracy value corresponds to the likeliness among the training and test data tuples. Hence, the pair-wise similarity of the data is determined as a result of prediction accuracy as depicted by Baldi et al. (2000).

The computation of sensitivity is given in equation (5.13), which determines the total positives, i.e., identifying the diabetic patients exactly. The computation of specificity is given in equation (5.14) that determines the total negatives, i.e., identifying the non-diabetic patients. The equations are given as follows:

$$\text{Accuracy} = \frac{(TP + TN)}{(TP + TN + FP + FN)} \tag{5.12}$$

$$\text{Sensitivity} = \frac{(\text{TP})}{(\text{TP} + \text{FN})} \tag{5.13}$$

$$\text{Specificity} = \frac{(\text{TN})}{(\text{TN} + \text{FP})} \tag{5.14}$$

This model uses ten-fold cross-validation for dividing the dataset into k number of subgroups. Each of the group is being tested across the classification scheme with the remaining set of $(k-1)$ subgroups.

As a result, k set of different test cases will be obtained for each of the training–test set arrangement, with its average providing the accuracy of the model. The metric kappa provides an arrangement among two sets of different observers with the same sort of data for qualitative items. The following signifies the property of kappa value:

- Value is 1 – whole agreement exists.
- Value is 0 – no or low level of agreement exists.

The kappa value in equation (5.17) can be calculated from the following equations:

$$k = \frac{p(A) - p(E)}{1 - p(E)} \tag{5.15}$$

$$p(A) = \frac{(\text{TP} + \text{TN})}{N} \tag{5.16}$$

$$p(E) = \frac{\left[(\text{TP} + \text{FN})(\text{TP} + \text{FP})(\text{TN} + \text{FN})\right]}{N} \tag{5.17}$$

Here, N corresponds to the total number of data tuples. $p(A)$ is the proportion of agreement with the classifier model, and the truth value is ascertained by equation (5.16). Also, the value $p(E)$ is the chance of agreement calculated by equation (5.17).

5.5.2 CONFUSION MATRIX

It corresponds to the matrix value across predicted and the actual value of the tuple of record that is classified. The prediction rate with the test data is provided in Table 5.3. With the use of the confusion matrix, one can easily identify the predicted value to that of the actual value. The comparison analysis of the performance metrics for type II diabetic dataset is illustrated in Figure 5.2, whereas an accuracy level is illustrated in Figure 5.3. Here,

1. TP is True Positive, i.e., Diabetic patients correctly diagnosed as Diabetic
2. FP is False Positive, i.e., Healthy people incorrectly identified as Diabetic

TABLE 5.3
Confusion Matrix

Prediction Value			Disease Specification	
	+	−		
Test value	+		True Positive rate (TP)	False Positive rate (FP)
	−		False Negative rate (FN)	True Negative rate (TN)

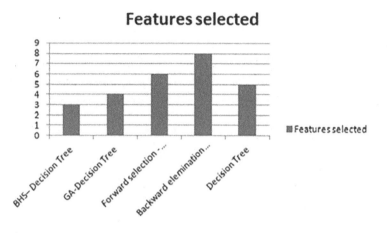

FIGURE 5.2 Comparison analyses of features selected among the algorithms for type II diabetic dataset.

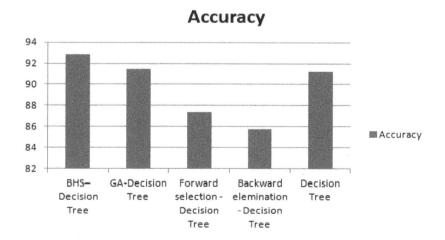

FIGURE 5.3 Comparison analyses of accuracy among the algorithms for type II diabetic dataset.

3. TN is True Negative, i.e., Healthy people correctly identified as healthy
4. FN is False Negative, i.e., Diabetic patients incorrectly identified as healthy

The evaluation has been made with various classification algorithms such as SVM, Neural Network, Decision Trees, Random Forest, and Naïve Bayes algorithms. Among the data classification scheme in combination with BHS algorithm, decision tree provided an improved level of accuracy than that of other algorithmic combinations upon iterations. So, decision tree is used for evaluating with BHS, and also the efficiency of decision tree algorithm is compared with other feature selection algorithms and the same has been tabulated in Table 5.5.

Similarly, the experimental analysis has been carried out for real-world heart disease dataset which contains 24 attributes and label with 306 records. Figures 5.4 and 5.5 provide the comparison analysis of algorithms and the accuracy levels obtained.

Also, the accuracy evaluation has been made with benchmark dataset such as cancer, Pima Indian diabetes, Cleveland heart disease dataset, and diabetic retinopathy dataset. Table 5.4 summarizes the accuracy level obtained with regard to benchmark dataset.

In consideration to the benchmark dataset, the performance of the proposed approach seems to be improved in accordance with heart disease and diabetic retinopathy datasets. Meanwhile, the attribute selection criterion needs to be improved. The attribute selection seems to be good for real-world dataset, as well as its performance both in the accuracy value and the attributes selected. In order to determine the attribute correlation and its dependency, the real-world type II diabetic dataset has been evaluated with an exhaustive evaluation in terms of parameter setting and the development of a linear model in accordance with the total number of features selected.

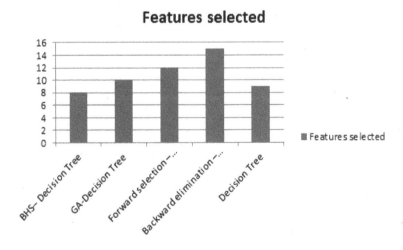

FIGURE 5.4 Comparison analyses of features selected among the algorithms for heart disease dataset.

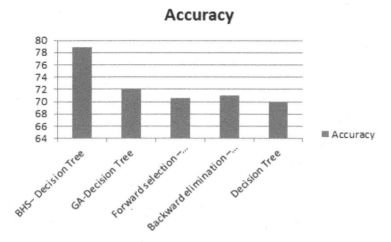

FIGURE 5.5   Comparison analyses of accuracy among the algorithms for heart disease dataset.

TABLE 5.4
Accuracy Level Obtained for Benchmark Dataset with the Proposed Approach

S.No.	Dataset	Total Records	Accuracy	Total Features	Features Selected
1	Pima Indian diabetes	394	75.4	8	5
2	Cancer	699	79.0	9	5
3	Cleveland heart disease	270	82.2	13	8
4	Diabetic retinopathy	1151	80.5	19	13

5.5.3   EXPERIMENTAL ANALYSIS WITH LINEAR MODEL DEVELOPMENT FOR TYPE II DIABETIC DATASET

5.5.3.1   Parameter Settings

The parameters for the feature selection are as follows: HMS = 10, HMCR = 0.8, PAR = 0.3, and the total number of iterations depends on the stopping criterion. The dataset initially consists of 732 instances with 10 attributes. Implementing the BHS-J48 algorithm on this dataset, after meeting the stopping criterion, only three features, namely PPG, A1c, MBG level, are found to be selected with a prediction accuracy of about 92.87% with an optimal solution in comparison with other algorithms as shown in Table 5.5. It has also been found that the age group greater than 30–50 has a specific impact on the influence of diabetes with respect to the mean glucose level. The level of PPG among the influenced people is equal to or more than 11.1 mmol/L (200 mg/dL).

The set of features selected has been incorporated with the experts in the domain of diabetes, and the final conclusion revealed that the model can be used efficiently

TABLE 5.5

Accuracy Level Obtained by the Proposed Method in Comparison with Other Algorithms

Algorithm	Accuracy	Features Selected
BHS – decision tree	92.87%	3
GA – decision Tree	91.42%	4
Forward selection – decision tree	87.32%	6
Backward elimination – decision tree	85.72%	8
Decision tree	91.17%	5

in the prediction of type II diabetes. Table 5.5 provides the accuracy levels obtained with the proposed method and the methods exist for predictive analysis with medical data.

5.5.3.2   Comparing the Efficacy of the Proposed Model with Existing Approaches

The efficacy of the proposed method has been compared with the implementation results obtained by the various authors. The comparison shows that the accuracy level obtained by the proposed method seems to be good with an improved accuracy of about 92.87% using a combination of three features. Table 5.6 provides the accuracy level obtained by various authors.

Upon analysis, most of the existing methods have been experimented with Pima Indian diabetic dataset. Some of the experiments have been carried out using decision trees; the efficacy of the proposed method seems to have higher accuracy with

TABLE 5.6

Accuracy level obtained by various authors

S.No.	Author	Dataset Used	Disease Specified	Algorithm Applied	Accuracy Level
1	Bioch et al. (1996)	Pima Indians Diabetes Dataset	Diabetes	Neural network and Bayesian approach	79.5%
2	Yue et al. (2008)	Pima Indians Diabetes Dataset	Type II Diabetes	WLS-SVM based on QPSO	95%
3	Han et al. (2008)	Pima Indians Diabetes Dataset	Diabetes	Decision Tree	72%
4	Barakat et al. (2010)	Real-world diabetic dataset	Diabetes Mellitus	Support Vector Machines (SVMs)	94%
5	Jarullah et al. (2011)	Pima Indians Diabetes Dataset	Diabetes	Decision Tree method	78.18%
6	Meng et al. (2013)	Real-world dataset from Guangzhou, China	Diabetes	Logistic Regression, Artificial neural networks (ANNs) and decision tree models	77.87%

less number of features selected. Also, the observed features are found to be dependent upon investigation from a medical expert. The following section provides the determination of correlation among the attributes with a linear mathematical model for risk analysis in type II diabetes.

5.5.3.3 Determination of Correlation among Risk using Linear Mathematical Model for Type II Diabetic Data

Regression analysis has been carried out for the determination of linearity among the predicted attributes PPG, A1c, and MBG level. The results obtained have been illustrated in Table 5.7.

In accordance with the selected feature, a detailed analysis has been made with the age group of the people with its corresponding parameter values. When considering age with PPG, the plot shows that the higher indication of age groups corresponds to 34–73 with a specified tolerance to PPG. Next, an analysis has been made between age and A1c values. It has been observed from Figures 5.6 and 5.7 that the age group

TABLE 5.7
Result of Regression Analysis

Attribute Name	Coefficients	Standard Error	t-Statistic
Significance level	0.010415		
AGE	−0.954	0.371	−2.571
PPG	260.794	20.42	12.769
Significance level	0.107734		
AGE	−0.186	0.115	−1.611
A1c	89.491	6.366	14.057
Significance level	0.761728		
AGE	0.035	0.116	0.3033
MBG	77.547	6.380	12.150

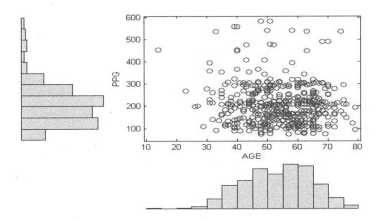

FIGURE 5.6   Comparisons among the data values between age and PPG.

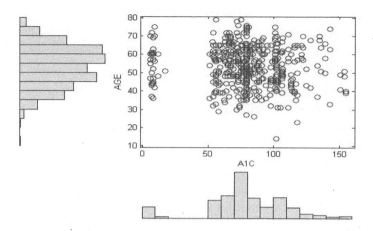

FIGURE 5.7   Comparisons among the data values between age and A1c.

corresponding to 40–67 has higher indication of A1c hemoglobin levels. Finally, the analysis has been made with age and MBG level, and it has been found that the age group 35–73 has been found to have higher glucose levels as depicted in Figure 5.8. In addition to the comparison of data values, a mathematical model has been developed in order to identify the strong correlation among the attributes. Table 5.8 provides the significance among the mathematical model of the attributes selected. The curve fitting with respect to the significance level among the selected attributes such as age with MBG level and A1c is shown in Figure 5.9, age with PPG and A1c is shown in Figure 5.10, and age with its MBG level and PPG is shown in Figure 5.11.

The linear mathematical relational model is defined as follows:

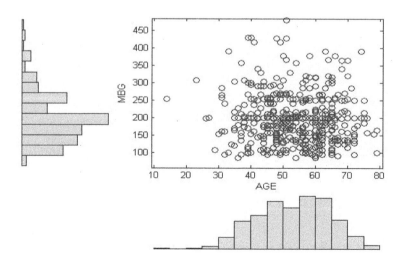

FIGURE 5.8   Comparisons among the data values between age and MBG.

TABLE 5.8

Significance Level and Linear Model among the Selected Attributes

S.No.	Comparison Between Attributes Selected	Significance Values			Goodness of Fit	R Square	RMSE
		P00	P10	P01			
1	Age vs. MBG and A1c	56.46	−0.0149	−0.007	Coefficient with 95%	0.00620	11.08
2	Age vs. PPG and A1c	57.07	−0.0071	−0.012	Coefficient with 95%	0.01336	11.04
3	Age vs. MBG and PPG	56.48	0.0032	−0.015	Coefficient with 95%	0.01331	11.04

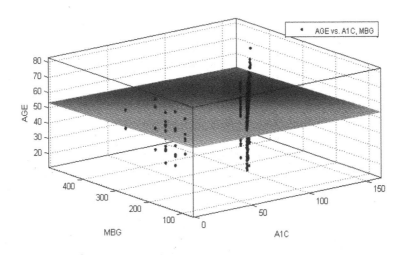

FIGURE 5.9 Significance level observed between age, MBG, and A1c.

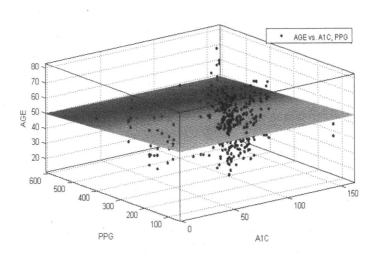

FIGURE 5.10 Significance level observed between age, PPG, and A1c.

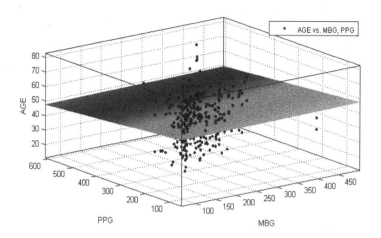

FIGURE 5.11　Significance level observed between age, PPG, and MBG.

$$f(x,y) = p_{00} + p_{10} \cdot x + p_{01} \cdot y \qquad (5.18)$$

The general modeled custom equation for all the selected attributes is defined as follows:

$$f(x,y) = a + b \cdot \sin(m \cdot pi \cdot x \cdot y) + c \cdot \exp\left(-(w \cdot y)^2\right) \qquad (5.19)$$

The coefficient values are observed to be

a = 53.6	b = 2.6	c = 0.88	m = 0.85	w = 0.9

The value of RMSE is found to be 11, which then statistically proves that the value is obtained in accordance with comparisons among all the attributes such as age, A1c, PPG, and MBG level, and hence, it has been statistically observed to be true for the attributes selected with the experimental data values.

From the experimental values, it has been learned that the attributes age, PPG, and MBG level have a strong relationship with its corresponding data values as observed in Figure 5.11. Hence, from the mathematical model, it is proved that the age, PPG, and MBG level depend upon another in determining diabetic nature for a given patient's health record.

Here, morbidity refers to the factors that contribute to the focus on death. The diseased state with its relevance is referred to as morbidity. Mortality refers to the number of occurrences of people who have died over the period of time in a group of population. In the proposed model, the data corresponds to the patients who have the occurrence of the disease with respect to type II diabetes. From the experimental results, with the selected set of risk factors, PPG and MBG levels are the contributing factors that refer to the people over the region of Theni, Tamil Nadu. If these factors are observed more clearly at the initial stage, then the number of deaths that arise due to the implication of the above risk factors gets reduced to a great extent. The model has been experimented for a new group of people with the medical experts at the medical college hospital for deployment. The results proved that the contributing factors are the main cause for the disease to occur over the region of Theni.

5.6 SUMMARY

This chapter deals with the investigation of type II diabetic risk factors using an improved combination of BHS with J48 decision tree algorithm. Concluding and comparing our findings, a predictive model has been developed which aims at facilitating the determination of major sort of risk factors for the disease concerned. The experimental results using the real-world dataset show that the proposed model can be used by physicians for the diagnosis and treatment of NCD with minimum number of clinical tests. With the exhaustive study of the data corresponding to type II diabetes, it has been observed that the age groups corresponding to 34–73 have been found to be more prevalent to the medium of type II diabetes, around the area with regard to location, likelihood, and dietary habits. The evaluation of the data model has been proved mathematically which then shows that the attributes age, PPG, and MBG level have more prevalence and strong correlation among one another. As a result, the selected set of attributes has a higher significance level in predicting type II diabetes.

REFERENCES

1. Gregers S. Andersen, Zaza Kamper-Jørgensen, Bendix Carstensen, Marie Norredam, Marie Norredam, Ib C. Bygbjerg, Marit E. Jørgensen, Marit E. Jørgensen. (2016). Diabetes among Migrants in Denmark: Incidence, Mortality, and Prevalence Based on a Longitudinal Register Study of the Entire Danish Population. *Diabetes Research and Clinical Practice*, 122, 9–16. doi:10.1016/J.DIABRES.2016.09.020
2. Jessica L. Browne, Giesje Nefs, Frans Pouwer, Jane Speight, Jane Speight. (2015). Depression, Anxiety and Self-Care Behaviours of Young Adults with Type 2 Diabetes: Results from the International Diabetes Management and Impact for Long-Term Empowerment and Success (MILES) Study. *Diabetic Medicine*, 32(1), 133–140. doi:10.1111/DME.12566
3. Jane Speight, Jessica L. Browne, John Furler. (2015). Testing Times! Choosing Wisely When It Comes to Monitoring Type 2 Diabetes. *The Medical Journal of Australia*, 203(9), 354–356. doi:10.5694/MJA15.00639
4. Ambady Ramachandran, Shobhana Ramachandran, Chamukuttan Snehalatha, Christina Augustine, Narayanasamy Murugesan, Vijay Viswanathan, Anil Kapur, Rhys Williams. (2007). Increasing Expenditure on Health Care Incurred by Diabetic Subjects in a Developing Country: a Study from India. *Diabetes Care*, 30(2), 252–256. doi:10.2337/DC06-0144
5. Shivam Agarwal. (2013). Data Mining: Data Mining Concepts and Techniques. 2013 *International Conference on Machine Intelligence and Research Advancement* [Internet]. 2013 Dec. doi:10.1109/icmira.2013.45

6. R. David, G. Leslie, Eric S. Kilpatrick. (2009). Translating the A1C Assay into Estimated Average Glucose Values: Response to Nathan et al. *Diabetes Care*, 32(1), e11. doi:10.2337/DC08-1524

7. Emirhan Gülçin Yıldırım, Adem Karahoca, Tamer Uçar. (2011). Dosage Planning for Diabetes Patients Using Data Mining Methods. *Procedia Computer Science*, 3, 1374–1380. doi:10.1016/J.PROCS.2011.01.018

8. Usha Ram, Usha Ram, Prabhat Jha, Patrick Gerland, Ryan J. Hum, Peter S. Rodriguez, Wilson Suraweera, Kaushalendra Kumar, Rajesh Kumar, Rajesh Dikshit, Denis Xavier, Rajeev Gupta, Prakash C. Gupta, Faujdar Ram. (2015). Age-Specific and Sex-Specific Adult Mortality Risk in India in 2014: Analysis of 0.27 Million Nationally Surveyed Deaths and Demographic Estimates from 597 Districts. *The Lancet Global Health*, 3(12), e767–e775. doi:10.1016/S2214-109X(15)00091-1

9. Shanthi Mendis, Stephen M. Davis, Bo Norrving. (2015). Organizational Update: The World Health Organization Global Status Report on Noncommunicable Diseases 2014; One More Landmark Step in the Combat against Stroke and Vascular Disease. *Stroke*, 46(5), 121–122. doi:10.1161/STROKEAHA.115.008097

10. David V. McQueen. (2013). *Global Handbook on Noncommunicable Diseases and Health Promotion*. Springer: New York, 481–481. doi:10.1007/978-1-4614-7594-1

11. Mohammad Danesh Zand, Amir Hossein Ansari, Caro Lucas, Reza Aghaee Zade Zoroofi. (2010). Risk Assessment of Coronary Arteries Heart Disease Based on Neuro-Fuzzy Classifiers. *2010 17th Iranian Conference of Biomedical Engineering (ICBME)* [Internet]. 2010 Nov. doi:10.1109/icbme.2010.5705028

12. Maja Atanasijević-Kunc, Jože Drinovec, Simona Ručigaj, Aleš Mrhar. (2011). Original Article: Simulation Analysis of Coronary Heart Disease, Congestive Heart Failure and End-Stage Renal Disease Economic Burden. *Mathematics and Computers in Simulation*, 82(3), 494–507. doi:10.1016/J.MATCOM.2010.10.024

13. Zong Woo Geem, Joong Hoon Kim, G. V. Loganathan. (2001). A New Heuristic Optimization Algorithm: Harmony Search. *Simulation*, 76(2), 60–68. doi:10.1177/003754970107600201

14. Xiaolei Wang, Xiao-Zhi Gao, Kai Zenger. (2014). An Introduction to Harmony Search Optimization Method. SpringerBriefs in Applied Sciences and Technology [Internet]. 2014 Jul 23; 1–4. doi:10.1007/978-3-319-08356-8_1

15. Jiawei Han, Micheline Kamber, Jian Pei. (2011). *Data Mining: Concepts and Techniques*. 3rd edition. The Morgan Kaufmann Series in Data Management Systems, Morgan Kaufmann Publishers, July 2011. ISBN 978-0123814791.

6 Predictive Analytics Using Particle Swarm Optimization with Decision Trees for Type II Diabetes

6.1 A REVIEW ON TYPE II DIABETES AND ITS IMPLICATIONS

Diabetes is a metabolic and chronic disease which is described by the prominent levels of blood glucose levels. Type II diabetes is the most common form of diabetes. With this form of diabetes, the body does not use insulin at proper levels. Hence, an insulin resistance is created which makes an oscillation in insulin levels. At time intervals, the human body can't make insulin at proper levels to keep the values of blood glucose at normal levels [1]. The prevalence of diabetes and its growth have been increasing enormously over all the regions in the world. The impact of diabetes caused about 1.5 million deaths in 2012, while higher values blood glucose added 2.2 million deaths with an increased risk of cardiac problems and other diseases. During this period, 80% of the disease occurred in low and middle age countries [2]. The World Health Organization (WHO) states that, during 2030, diabetes will be one among the major causes of death in various regions of the world. In 2014, about 422 million adults (merely 8.5% of the total population) were affected due to diabetes as compared to 4.7% in 1980. The problem of diabetes may lead to stroke, heart attack, kidney failure, blindness, and limp difficulty [3].

According to a study made by the Indian Diabetes Foundation, in India, about 63 million people suffer from possible disability which is expected to rise up to 80 million during the year 2025. The survey made by Dr. Anoop Misra states that about 37% of the urban south Indians suffer due to diabetes and pre-diabetes. The work by them provides a statistical report from the year of 1965 to 2005 that conveys segregation among urban and rural population having diabetes. The report states that there is a significant increase in urban area with an exponential trend $R^2 = 0.74$ and a slower range in the rural area with $R^2 = 0.28$. The statistics reveal that the ratio of the population with diabetes varies from 5.4% in the northern region and 12.3%–15.5% in Chennai zone and to a range of 16.8% in central India as stated by Gupta and Misra (2007). The prevalence of diabetes is depicted in Figure 6.1.

The intersection among medical science and information technology provides a solution toward data-driven decision-making. The future community is in need of an

DOI: 10.1201/9781003330189-6

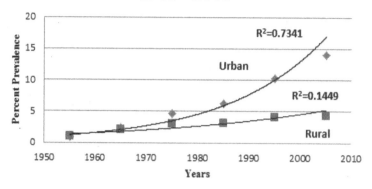

FIGURE 6.1   Prevalence of diabetes in India 1965–2005.

integrated access to clinical information to formulate computer-based data management and decision-making process. Hence, it provides the way not only for managing electronic health records which engage clinical and patient information but also for obtaining a data model which supports in deciding proper levels. The process of decision-making includes major components such as the data elements (attributes), measurement levels, stopping criteria, test process, and the implications of the attribute level with its corresponding process. Population-based healthcare study will provide the significant features that are more predominant in the disease. The significance of disease-specific syndromes with the location of the people could solve the problems of the origins and progress of the disease over the regions [4]. The notable benefits with healthcare data analytics and feature selection include the following:

1. Reducing clinical cost
2. Providing a decision support model
3. Risk determination with specific reference to locality, likelihood, and dietary habits
4. Healthcare coordination
5. Improvement in patient monitoring systems

Different sorts of prediction models have been deployed in the medical field which serve as the backbone for disease management and diagnosis. Most of the techniques related to supervised learning techniques are in practice for clinical prediction. Some of them include linear regression model, logistic regression, neural network, decision trees, and survival data models. These techniques focus on the significance and nature of the data, which then provide the relationship among the features and between the features over the target variable. Among the various models, choosing the suitable one for the particular healthcare problem depends upon the nature of the data and the relationship that exists between the attributes. There are various forms of algorithmic methods; however some focus only on feature selection and others only on data classification. Algorithms used in the existing system are Multi-agent PSO, Genetic algorithm, Support Vector Machine classifiers, k-means clustering, logistic regression, decision trees, Naïve Bayes, and sensitivity and specificity measures. These methods have been used explicitly for either classification or prediction. The major limitations observed are:

1. There seems to be no form of improvement in the operating parameters of the existing algorithms.
2. Most of the methods have been dealt with benchmark dataset rather than focusing on real-world data.
3. The application of feature selection and classification methods for real-world dataset in medical informatics lags in accordance with risk determination and analysis.

The proposed research work in this chapter focuses upon the development of an algorithmic method using PSO with its improvement in operating parameters utilizing decision tree algorithm. Data corresponding to type II diabetes from a regional hospital were used in developing the algorithmic model. The operating characteristics of PSO algorithm depend upon the fixing of inertial weight in accordance with the number of iterations and population generation. The efficiency of the PSO algorithm depends upon the phenomenon of inertial weight adjustment in accordance with particles position and its velocity. In order to make the particles accelerate for an optimal solution and to improve the comprehensibility of the model in the given search space, we have proposed a scheme for fixing a self-adaptive inertial weight with modified convergence logic. This mechanism makes the particle accelerate in its logical space to show a variation in each set of iteration at individual levels. With this, the movement of the particle is assigned with a small or larger value of inertial weight.

Once the features are selected, the fitness function is evaluated with the total number of positive and negative cases which have been predicted by the decision tree algorithm. The efficiency of the method is tested with Fisher's Linear Discriminant Analysis, which includes test case interpretation and evaluation. The correlation between the selected features is determined using curve fitting by an exponential distribution using R^2 analysis. Table 6.1 describes the accuracy level, data used, and model evaluated by various authors.

Based on the limitations and drawbacks of the existing techniques about algorithmic model and utilization of real-world dataset, there is a need for an optimal algorithm that encompasses feature selection and data classification with an improvement toward convergence speed, accuracy, and execution time. In order to overcome the drawbacks, we have proposed an improved combination of PSO algorithm with decision trees for the assessment of risk factors that correspond to type II diabetes.

6.2   RATIONALE BEHIND THE PROPOSED APPROACH

Data optimization methods are deployed in various fields such as engineering, medical sciences, management, physical sciences, and social learning. The process behind optimization is to choose the best solution from the set of feasible solutions

TABLE 6.1

Literature Survey Over Medical Data by Various Authors

S.No.	Author	Year	Disease Specified	Algorithm Applied	Dataset Used	Accuracy Level (%)
1	Karaolis et al.	2010	Coronary Heart Disease	Decision Trees	Real-world Heart disease dataset (European People)	75.00
2	Patil et al.	2010	Diabetes	K-means clustering with C4.5 Decision Trees	Pima Indians Diabetes Data Set	92.38
3	Sahu and Mishra	2012	Cancer	PSO with SVM, KNN	Benchmark cancer dataset	96.00
4	Xue et al.	2014	Lung	PSO with SVM	Lung UCI	78.40
5	Tang et al.	2015	Non-communicable	MAPSO	Benchmark data	92.25
6	Lee and Kim	2016	Type II diabetes	Naïve Bayes with logistic regression	Real-world diabetic dataset (Korean people)	73.50
7	West et al.	2016	Type II diabetes	Sensitivity and Specificity with Monte Carlo and Hypercube model	Real-world diabetic data from rural Tanzania	-
8	Low et al.	2017	Kidney disease with type II diabetes	Stepwise multi-variable logistic regression	Real-world diabetic data from a regional hospital	75.60

thereby providing scientific decision-making. The problem formulation in optimization includes identifying the decision variables, objective function, and learning factors which correspond to the analysis of the feature selection process. The next is to choose an appropriate numerical method to solve, test, and make proper decision for the optimal solution obtained. There are various optimization methods and some of them are enumeration methods, gradient methods, random search methods, and meta-heuristic methods. Table 6.2 presents the summary corresponding to the limitations and usage of the optimization methods.

The advantage of meta-heuristic method over enumeration, gradient-based, and random search methods is that it corresponds to an iterative process with subordinate heuristic with a combination of different intellectual concepts for exploring and exploiting the given search space [5]. These methods are stochastic in nature, with random search corresponding to local and global best solution for the given search space [6]. There are various meta-heuristic methods such as genetic algorithm, evolution strategy, tabu search, differential evolution, and swarm intelligence methods.

TABLE 6.2

Comparison among Optimization Methods

S.No.	Method	Limitations	Usage
1	Enumeration methods	It requires high computation cost and provides finite feasible solution	Generally used to solve integer programming and combinatorial problems
2	Gradient methods	These methods belong to local search techniques and provides only local optimal solution	It is used to fix the search space which is proportional to the positive or negative gradient of the function
3	Random search methods	These methods can be used in cases when the objective function is not continuous or differentiable	Easy to apply for complex problems without gradient information
4	Meta-heuristic methods	Meta-heuristic algorithms perform differently in different types of applications. Statistical data analysis will justify its performance	Meta-heuristic methods can be used as common framework that can be applied to different problems with modifications to adapt to the specific problem

When compared to other methods, the major advantage of swarm intelligence technique is: these methods have the ability to act in a coordinated way without the presence of a controller (coordinator). The applications of swarm intelligence focus on the behavior of ants, flocking of birds, swarm-based network, and the behavior of wasps.

Among all the techniques in the swarm intelligence, PSO is a population-based intelligent system that requires initial population corresponding to random solutions. The search for the optimal solution is obtained by updating the particle generations without any external evolution operators such as selection, crossover, and mutation. The particles in PSO fly over the given search space and learn accordingly with their own experiences with the velocity, which is then provided with cognition factor, social factor, and inertial weight. The fixing up of target value for inertial weight plays a major role in the exploration of the search space to find a near-optimal solution, which is the major contribution in this research work.

From the literature, it is noted that researchers in medical informatics focused on either feature selection or data classification in medical data prediction. Also, the utilization of statistical measurements is limited to sensitivity, specificity, F-measure, and Receiver Operating Curve (ROC) analysis. Hence, there should be an algorithmic method that focuses on feature selection, classification, and statistical analysis in medical data for exploring the risk factors that contribute to the disease.

Data classification and prediction play significant roles in risk factor determination and its relationship. Among all classification techniques, decision trees have the unique ability to assign definite values to a given problem, decision with the outcome of reducing ambiguity in the decision-making process. The following are the specific characteristics that correspond to the selection of decision tree for our algorithmic model development with an improved combination of PSO algorithm:

• Specificity
• Comprehensive nature
• Transparency
• Flexibility
• Resilience
• Data validation

With the specific characteristics, the decision tree provides a framework in order to quantify the observed values and the probabilistic function of each possible outcome of a decision. This phenomenon makes data solvers and decision-makers to have a good choice in data classification with that of available alternatives.

6.3   PROPOSED METHOD USING PSO-J48

6.3.1   ALGORITHM DESCRIPTION

The proposed model encompasses the procedure of feature selection paradigm using PSO with J48 (Java Implementation of C4.5 Decision Tree algorithm). PSO is one of the biologically inspired algorithms that are stimulated by the behavior of bird flocking [7]. PSO is a computational procedure that fundamentally centers toward optimizing a given problem in an iterative way to infer a sensibly ideal arrangement. The generated particles are accelerated with an initial velocity. The movement of each of the particles is determined by the particles pbest. The assurance of the best particle over the signified fitness function is dictated by the gbest value. The entire search space is updated by the position obtained by each particle over the iterations [8]. The particles are accelerated to reach the optimal solution until the stopping criterion is reached as examined [9]. In general, PSO is a meta-heuristic algorithm that targets the determination of optimal solution for a given measure of quality. It does not use the derivatives in the selection of functions for the defined variables. The basic concept of PSO lies in accelerating each particle toward its pbest and the gbest locations, with a random weighted acceleration at each time step. The search space exploration is illustrated in Figure 6.2. Each particle tries to modify its position using the following information:

1. The current positions
2. The current velocities
3. The distance between the current position and pbest
4. The distance between the current position and gbest

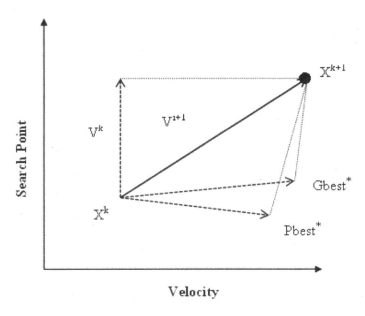

FIGURE 6.2   PSO search space in an environment.

The modification of the particle's position during iteration can be mathematically modeled according to the following equation:

$$V_i^{k+1} = wV_i^k + c_1 \text{Rand}_1 \times (\text{pbest}_i - s_i^k) + c_2 \text{Rand}_2 \times (\text{gbest} - s_i^k) \qquad (6.1)$$

where V_i^{k+1} is the weighting factor with new velocity at an iteration $k + 1$, V_i^k is the weighting factor with current velocity at an iteration k, w is the inertial weighting function, Rand is the random number which is uniformly distributed between the ranges of [0–1], s_i^k is the current position of the particle for the iteration k, pbest_i is the best position reached by the particle I, gbest is the global best position observed from the group of particles for the given iteration, and c_1, c_2 are learning factors.

The weighting function for the exploration of the particles needs to be determined in accordance with the particle's initial and final positions. The mechanism of inertial weight follows a global search strategy and smaller inertial weight with local search strategy [10]. The size of the group for the set of particles has to be assigned, which is defined by the factor N. Then, the generation of the initial population has to be made, which ranges from $x_1, x_2, x_3 \ldots \ldots \ldots x_N$, and the particles are accelerated with an initial velocity to reach its first new position, which is given as $x_1(1), x_2(1), x_3(1) \ldots \ldots \ldots x_N(1)$. The corresponding vector values are $x_i(1) = \{1, 2, 3 \ldots \ldots N\}$ which are referred to as the vector coordinates of the particle. The objective function for the particles is given by $f[x_1(1)], f[x_2(1)], f[x_3(1)] \ldots \ldots f[x_N(1)]$. The observed particles move accordingly to obtain a merely optimal solution with the triggered velocity updated at each level of iteration [11]. The operation of the particle position can be made by the following equation:

$$P_i^{k+1} = P_i^k + V_i^{k+1} \qquad (6.2)$$

where P_i^k is the current position of the particle i at iteration k and V_i^{k+1} is the updated velocity of the particle i at iteration k

During iteration at each level, the particle finds its best position over the entire set of movements, and hence, it is referred to as the particles pbest value. Among the overall particles' movements and iterations, the observed best value (the best particle's position) is referred to as the gbest value. The values c_1 and c_2 are the cognitive learning factors that influence the social group. If the observed solution is convergent, then the iteration gets stopped [12]. The determination of the convergence at a point of contact can be ascertained by the following conditions:

1. The termination is made when maximum number of iterations is reached as specified.
2. Once the solution is acceptable, the iterations can be terminated.
3. If there is no improvement over the generation of swarms, then the process can be terminated.
4. If the swarm radius is closer to zero, the condition gets terminated.
5. If the slope of the objective function is close to zero, then the condition gets terminated.

The new position that has been determined must be away from the gbest and pbest positions. Only then the velocity of the particle ranges widely to a high value. The set of selected features is fed as an input to the J48. The J48 algorithm classifies the input features based upon the splitting criterion that has been used for evaluation in the determination of the accuracy over the selected set of features. The algorithm proceeds following the input parameters:

1. Training data partition (D)
2. The attribute list
3. Attribute splitting criterion that determines the best splitting partition.

There are various forms of attribute selection measures such as information gain and Gini index. If the data records are segregated in a binary format, then we can use Gini index as an attribute selection measure. But for our dataset, the values for each of the attributes seem to be continuous and discrete rather than binary valued. Therefore, the information gain is used for the best splitting criterion in creating the tree. The information to classify a tuple is represented in the following equation:

$$\text{Info}(D) = -\sum_{i-1}^{m} p_i \log_2(p_i) \qquad (6.3)$$

The information to be obtained after the partition is given by the following equation:

$$\text{Info}_A(D) = \sum_{j-1}^{v} \frac{|D_j|}{|D|} \times \text{Info}(D_j) \qquad (6.4)$$

The recursive partitioning ends when any one of the following conditions is reached:

1. If all the tuples of record belong to the same class in D.
2. If there occur no attributes for further partition.
3. If there occur no tuples for an identified branch during partition.

With the generated set of particles for each of the iteration, the subset of features is validated for its functional value in which each set is used up for training and testing over J48 classifier. As a result, the fitness for each of the particles is evaluated. During iteration for the particles, the best fitness is the local best fitness value, which is used as the current fitness for the particle generated over time. The local best position for the first iteration is the current position for the particle; if the local best position of that particle is nearer to the convergence point in the search space when compared to the previous stage, then the position gets updated to the highest value over further iterations.

The global fitness value is then the maximum of the local best value observed so far for each set of iteration is concerned. The process continues until the convergence in the search space is reached. During iteration, the position and the velocity of the particles get updated simultaneously. The fitness is evaluated using J48 classifier under the following conditions:

1. If the current fitness is lesser than that of the local best fitness value
2. If the current fitness is lesser than that of the global best fitness value

Then, the global best fitness is set to be the current fitness, or else the position and velocity of the particle get updated each time. At last, when the stopping criterion is met, the procedure ends. With the number of tuples classified, if the class label of the nth tuple of the records is the same as that of the class label of the positive test case of the tuple, then the value of True Positive (TP) gets incremented accordingly. Similarly, if the test cases of the negative tuple match with those of the classified tuple, then the value of the negative tuple gets incremented. The fitness value is calculated by the addition of correctly classified positive and negative tuples to that of the total number of records. Procedure 6.1 provides the PSO algorithmic process in locating the best solution for the given search space.

Procedure 6.1 Workflow of proposed PSO-J48 model

01: initiate

02: **for** i=1 to the quantity of the particles

03: the velocity and position of the particle is initialized randomly

04: **end for**

05: **do**

06: **for** i=1 to the number of particles

07: Compute the fitness value of the swarm by J48 ()

08: **if** the observed fitness value is superior to pbest then assign it as new pbest for iterations

09: **end if**

10: **end for**

11: Select the swarm with the best fitness for all particles to be gbest

12: **for** i =1 to the number of particle swarms

13: The new velocity of particle swarm i at iteration k is considered as in equation (6.2)

14: The location of particle swarm i at an iteration k is rationalized as in equation (6.3)

15: **end for**

16: **while** (stopping condition is not met)

17: **end**

Pseudo code of J48 algorithm:

01: **start**

02: **for** x =1 to the total number of training tuples and its corresponding class labels

03: **for** m =1 to the total sum of candidate attributes

04: Specify a splitting measure (Information gain/Gain ratio/Gini index)

05: **end for**

06: **end for**

07: Create a node N_d

08: **if** all of the records in training data have same output class value C

09: **then**

10: return N_d as a leaf node with class label C.

11: **if** attr_list = {empty}, **then**

Return N_d as a leaf node labeled with major of class values.

Apply splitting criterion measure

Make node N_d with the splitting criterion.

Remove the splitting criterion attribute from the attr_list.

12: **for** each value i in the splitting criterion attribute.

13: D_i = no. of observations in training dataset satisfying attribute value i.

14: **if** D_i is empty **then**

15: attach a leaf node labeled with majority class output value to node N_d.

16: **else**

Attach the node returned by decision tree to node N_d.

17: **end if**

18: **end for**

19: return node N_d

20: **end if**

21: **end if**

26: **for** i = 1 to number of training tuples (N)

27: **if** Class$_i$ = Predicted Class$_i$ of testing data **then**

28: **if** Class$_i$ = Class label of positive tuples **then**

29: TP = TP + 1

30: **else if** Class$_i$ = Class label of negative tuples **then**

31: TN = TN + 1

32: **end if**

33: **end if**

34: **end for**

35: Fitness function = $(\text{TP} + \text{TN/N})$

36: end

6.3.2 PROPOSED WORKFLOW

The modules corresponding to the proposed workflow are data collection, data pre-processing, feature selection, classification, and model evaluation. Data collection involves the retrieval of dataset related to type II diabetes such as patient's data, blood sample data, and its comorbidities. Then, by utilizing the data analysis, the valuable information (patterns) from the dataset can be retrieved. The collected diabetes dataset corresponding to various sorts of events such as pre-diabetes, Type I diabetes, and type II diabetes is segregated by assigning class labels to each of the corresponding patient record. From the set of records, the optimized feature set is identified by applying PSO with the proposed self-adaptive inertial weight by modified convergence logic. With the selected set of features, the fitness function is calibrated using J48 algorithm.

Among the variants of the decision tree classifier, the J48 has been found to be an improved one from the experiments [13]. For the initial phase of the iteration process, the particle's local fitness has to be estimated which is then assigned as the current fitness of the particle. Among all the observed local positions, the best position is chosen to be the current position of the particle as suggested. At each level, in updating the particle position and velocity values, the fitness of the particle is evaluated using the J48 classifier. The workflow of the proposed model is illustrated in Figure 6.3. The set of classified tuples of records will then be observed from the confusion matrix with true positive, true negative, false positive, and false negative. The grouping among the set of positive and negative tuples of records is calculated as per the process described in Figure 6.4.

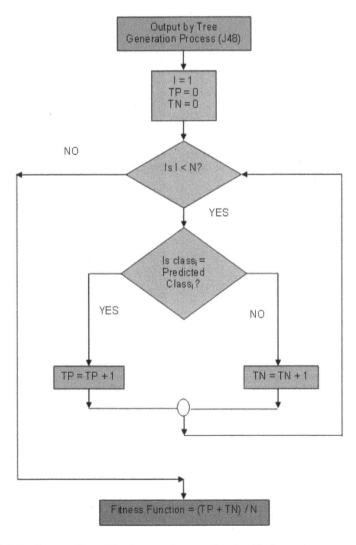

FIGURE 6.3 Computation of the fitness value over the classified records.

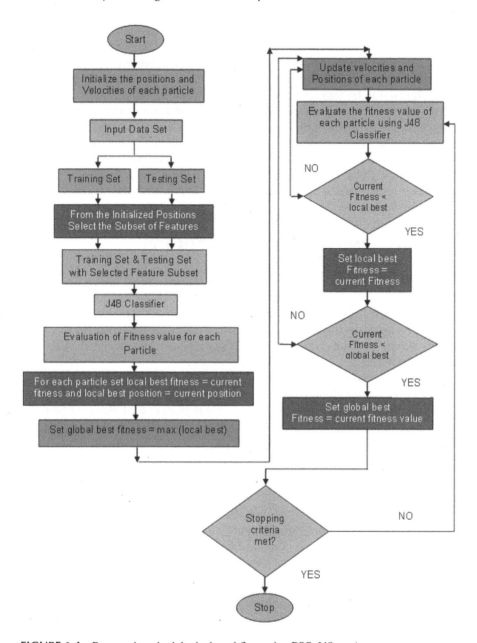

FIGURE 6.4   Proposed methodological workflow using PSO-J48.

With the generated set of particles for each of the iteration, the subset of features is validated for its functional value in which each set is used for training and testing over J48 classifier [14]. As a result, the fitness for each of the sets will be evaluated. During iteration over the set of particles, the best fitness is the local best fitness value, which is used as the current fitness for the particle generated over time. The local best position for the first iteration is the current position for the particle if the local best position of that particle is nearer to the convergence point in the search space. When compared to the previous stage, the position gets updated to the highest one over further iteration. The global fitness value is then the maximum of the local best value observed so far for each set of iterations. The process gets continued until the convergence in the search space is found to be elevated. For each of the iterations, the position and the velocity of the particles get updated simultaneously. The fitness is evaluated using J48 classifier under the condition if the current fitness is lesser than that of local best fitness and also the current fitness is lesser than the global best fitness. Then, the global best fitness is set to be the current fitness, or else the position and velocity of the particle get updated each time. At last, when the stopping criterion is met, the procedure ends.

6.4 EXPERIMENTAL RESULTS AND DISCUSSION

6.4.1 LEARNING POPULATION

A total of 732 subjects were collected for the period of 2012–2015 under the examination of a medical expert. Written informed permission was obtained from the medical experts for the medical study. The subjected data were pre-processed according to the mechanism of data cleaning, identifying duplicates, and making the data suitable for processing.

To handle the numeric data values appropriate for data analysis, the values have been signified to the min-max range with zero mean or Z-Score data standardization technique. In this method, the working principle is given in the following equation:

$$Z = \frac{X_i - \mu}{\sigma} \tag{6.5}$$

where X_i is the value of the attribute A, μ is the mean value, and σ is the standard deviation.

The observed data contains the data attributes pertaining to the comorbidities, informative patterns, and pre-diabetic nature corresponding to type II diabetes. From the set of observed records, an optimized feature set is determined using PSO and J48. Finally, the data tuples and their associated class labels with optimized features get examined and analyzed by medical practitioners. With the observed model, the existence of type II diabetes and its risk can be evaluated by medical experts.

6.4.2 ATTRIBUTE DESCRIPTION AND MEASUREMENT

The processed medical data have 23 attributes including the class label as described in Section 3.2.2. Each of the defined attributes has its exact specification level of normal, pre-diabetics condition, and the occurrence of diabetes. The range values for each of the attributes vary significantly for male and female subjects who are prone to type II diabetes. The ascertained values have been signified according to the Diabetic Association of India and WHO.

6.4.3   PSO Operating Parameters and Learning Factors

In the development of the prediction model using PSO-J48, for the execution of PSO for the defined number of iterations needs, the parameter has to be definite. There are about two learning factors C_1 and C_2 (cognition and social learning factors) which have to be fixed during the calculation of the fitness function. The cognition factor is defined as $C_1 r_{i,n}^j \left(P_{i,n}^j - X_{i,n}^j \right)$ which represents the own particles experience. The social learning factor then reflects the evidence shared by all the particles as expressed by $C_2 r_{i,n}^j \left(G_{i,n}^j - X_{i,n}^j \right)$. The learning factors play a significant role in exploring the particle in the given search space [15]. If the values of C_1 and $C_2 = 0$, then there exists no cognition and social learning for the particles about velocity updates. Therefore, we can't observe an optimal solution unless the solution is on its path of observance. Upon the condition for C_1 to be 0, the consequence for velocity update is known to be the 'social' only learning model. By having an interaction between the particles, the PSO has its ability to formulate into a new search space. Due to this behavior, the particles converge to a faster speed of action. The solution might be successful for some of the test cases upon performance analysis.

When $C_2 = 0$, there occurs no social learning among the particles about velocity update. Hence, the search for the best position is not shared as information among the particles. Therefore, unless information has been shared among the particles across the individuals, each one of the particles is said to run independently. Upon these conditions, the algorithm is said to have slower convergence rate than that of the previous one similar to the experiments [16]. About the learning factors C_1 and C_2, the PSO has its operating parameter which is said to be the inertial weight. If the inertial weight for the particles is not fed for the particles in searching the best position, then the velocity of the particles is said to be memory-less with the faster convergence factor than the original form of PSO. Hence, without inertial weight, the particles have their ability to sample their positions in and around the *pbest* and *gbest* values. The values corresponding to C_1 and C_2 are set to 2 as recommended by Kennedy and Eberhart [16]. The reason for setting $C_1 = C_2 = 2$ is that the social and cognition learning has the same effect on velocity update.

An interconnected group is formed among the individuals with a significant coordination and adaptability by communal attraction among the members. Collective behavior ascends without unified control. Members in the environment act according to that of the local behavior between them in order to provide a collective pattern. The learning behavior produces a global pattern from the rules learned among the individuals in a self-organizing conduct.

Disseminating the collective behavior among the individuals in the group is a difficult task and it won't be consistent all the time. The process of making the individuals learn behavior in a local group depends upon the parameters and empirical observations. To characterize the behavior of the individuals in the group, an appropriate mathematical model is essential with its observed quantitative analysis.

6.4.4 MODIFIED SELF-ADAPTIVE INERTIAL WEIGHT WITH CONVERGENCE LOGIC

Since each of the particles associated with the swarm has inherited variant differences in each state of iteration, it is logical to have self-adaptive inertial weight at the individual level. In accordance with the particle behavior of mechanics, the velocity update is expressed as follows:

$$V_{i,n+1}^j = wV_{i,n}^j + F_{i,n}^j \qquad (6.6)$$

where

$$F_{i,n}^j = C_1 r_{i,n}^j \left(P_{i,n}^j - X_{i,n}^j \right) + C_2 r_{i,n}^j \left(G_{i,n}^j - X_{i,n}^j \right) \qquad (6.7)$$

The value of $F_{i,n}^j$ represents the acceleration of the particle as it moves toward the region of $P_{i,n}^j$ and G_n^j in the given search space. If the regions of $V_{i,n}^j$ and $F_{i,n}^j$ pointing in different directions, then the particle is said to lie far away from the optimal region of $P_{i,n}^j$ and G_n^j respectively. As a result, the particle is said to modify its jth component for velocity, and the corresponding inertial weight $w_{i,n}^j$ should be set to a smaller value. In another way, smaller values of $V_{i,n}^j$ and $F_{i,n}^j$ imply that it is not crucial to modify the particle velocity and the value of $w_{i,n}^j$ can be set to a larger value. The acceleration of the particle in accordance with the convergence speed and the fixation of inertial weight are subject to the following conditions:

- If the values of $V_{i,n}^j$ and $F_{i,n}^j$ are large, then the jth component is in the correct direction, and it is said to speed up the inertial weight which is then set to a larger value of index.
- If the values of $V_{i,n}^j$ and $F_{i,n}^j$ are small, then the jth component of the particle is in near-optimal position, and the weight is set to a smaller value of index.

Upon these conditions, the convergence of the particle is assigned in accordance with particle's position and its movement in velocity. Therefore, the value of $w_{i,n}^j$ is considered to be the function of $\left| F_{i,n}^j \right|$ and $\left| V_{i,n}^j \right|$. The incorporation of the inertial weight factor is depicted in equation 6.6 and the value of $F_{i,n}^j$ is depicted in equation 6.7. The value of inertial weight can be chosen accordingly with the linear or non-linear function of the number of iterations. Table 6.3 describes various stages of inertial weights with regard to the number of iterations and accuracy.

   It has been observed that with inertial weight for value 0.9, the estimated accuracy is found to be 98.60% with external calibrated iteration value of 6 with detailed internal estimates for the iteration value six which are tabulated in Table 6.3 with all the observed parametric measures. The highest accuracy value, kappa, WMR, WMP, correlation with minimum classification error, absolute error, and Root-Mean-Squared error (RMSe) are obtained for the specific particle number that is highlighted in Table 6.4. Literature experiences for the choice of inertial weight have also been analyzed over the benchmark data. For the benchmark cases, the values for the inertial weight have been varied below 0.8 and above 1.2. The exploration ability of the algorithm is found to be worse than that of the original PSO algorithm.

TABLE 6.3
Selection of Inertial Weight with Improvement in Accuracy

S.No.	Iteration	Inertial Weight Values	Accuracy
1	1	0.4	76.54
2	2	0.5	81.86
3	3	0.6	87.32
4	4	0.7	92.21
5	5	0.8	96.84
6	6	0.9	98.60
7	7	1.0	97.24
8	8	1.1	93.00
9	9	1.2	90.84
10	10	1.3	89.96

When the values of w are fixed between 0.8 and 1.2, the algorithm has a better way for search space exploration to fix the global optimum solution with a minimum number of iterations. The experimental work by [16] also states that the range for inertial weight values has been given a significant improvement over the performance of PSO algorithm in a decreased level of time with iterations. The level of decreasing factor concerning time for inertial weight is given in the following equation:

$$w_n = \frac{(w_{initial} - w_{final})(n_{max} - n)}{n_{max} + w_{final}} \tag{6.8}$$

where w_n is the value corresponding to inertial weight at the nth iteration, $w_{initial}$ is the initial value of inertial weight, w_{final} is the final value of inertial weight, n is the iteration number, and n_{max} is the maximum iteration number.

Massive forms of experimental investigations have been made by [17] in accordance with decreasing variations of inertial weight. The convergence rate of PSO algorithm is not sensitive toward the number of iterations and the population size. Also, it is to be importantly noted that PSO algorithm may lack global search capability if the value of the chosen inertial weight is small. Therefore, as a consequence, PSO algorithm can be solved with the dynamic forms of real-world applications. $Rand_1$ and $Rand_2$ are the particle generation random numbers, each of which is set to the value around $[0-1]$, respectively. During iteration, the particle's best position is determined by the value of pbest and the best value obtained so far by some particle is gbest for the given set of population [18]. Once the features are selected, the accuracy is determined using the classifier by formulating test and training datasets. The validation of the model is set to 10-fold for the mechanism of cross-validation. Hence, the one part of the entire data is used up for test phase, and the remaining nine parts are used for the training phase. The execution continues until all the segments of the tuples are evaluated for cross-validation.

TABLE 6.4
Observed Measures for Performance Metrics

S.No.	Particle Number	Accuracy (%)	Classification Error (%)	Kappa	WMR (%)	WMP (%)	Absolute Error	RMS Error	Correlation
1	0	91.40	8.60	0.809	90.12	91.36	0.106	0.266	0.814
2	1	91.00	9.00	0.803	89.44	91.19	0.115	0.265	0.806
3	2	92.00	8.00	0.824	90.95	91.77	0.102	0.255	0.827
4	3	96.40	3.60	0.922	96.34	95.93	0.037	0.157	0.923
5	4	89.80	10.20	0.771	87.29	90.51	0.146	0.3	0.777
6	5	96.40	3.60	0.922	96.34	96.01	0.042	0.165	0.923
7	6	91.00	9.00	0.804	90.17	90.44	0.111	0.283	0.806
8	7	91.00	9.00	0.805	90.17	90.63	0.109	0.281	0.808
9	8	94.80	5.20	0.886	94.11	94.68	0.066	0.199	0.888
10	9	95.60	4.40	0.903	94.98	95.61	0.052	0.174	0.906
11	10	91.00	9.00	0.801	89.32	91.31	0.114	0.275	0.806
12	11	95.20	4.80	0.897	95.28	94.89	0.049	0.168	0.901
13	12	91.80	8.20	0.816	89.70	92.83	0.117	0.260	0.824
14	13	93.20	6.80	0.853	92.5	93.19	0.079	0.221	0.857
15	14	95.80	4.20	0.909	95.62	95.32	0.049	0.175	0.909
16	15	92.60	7.40	0.837	91.42	92.75	0.103	0.240	0.841
17	16	89.20	10.80	0.760	87.19	89.63	0.150	0.310	0.767
18	17	98.60	1.40	0.970	98.66	98.37	0.015	0.071	0.970
19	18	90.00	10.00	0.776	87.69	90.54	0.137	0.295	0.782
20	19	88.80	11.20	0.756	87.73	88.06	0.142	0.315	0.758

6.4.5 METRICS FOR EVALUATION

The performance of the method is evaluated through the following metrics:

Accuracy: If we use the entire set of training data to model classifier performance, then the observed result would be optimistic in nature. For our problem, we validate the model with the test data tuples. These test tuples, which are independent of the training data tuples, are being randomly selected. Meanwhile, these test tuples are not for modeling the classifier; rather, they are used to estimate the classifier performance. The accuracy of a classifier is defined as the percentage of test data tuples that have been correctly classified by the classifier. The label concerned with each of the tuples in a test data record is compared with that of the learned classifier class prediction for the tuple [19]. The evaluation of accuracy is estimated as follows:

$$\text{Accuracy} = \left(\frac{TP + TN}{TP + TN + FP + FN} \right) \tag{6.9}$$

Classification error: The classification error in a classifier model is defined as the total number of incorrectly classified instances or tuples of record during evaluation. The total number of misclassified instances defined the error rate of the developed model in the following equation:

$$E_i = \left(\frac{n}{N} \right) \tag{6.10}$$

where n is the total number of tuples incorrectly classified and N is the total number of tuples in the given dataset of record.

Kappa statistics: It is a measure of the degree of nonrandom agreement between observers or measurements of the same categorical variable. The calculation is given in the following equation:

$$K = \left(\frac{p(A) - p(E)}{1 - p(E)} \right) \tag{6.11}$$

Weighted mean recall (WMR) and weighted mean precision (WMP): F-score is a statistical measure of test accuracy which considers both precision p and recall r to determine the score value. The value p determines the fraction of retrieved instances that are relevant, while r determines the fraction of relevant instances that are retrieved. The measure is given in the following equations:

$$\text{precision} = \left(\frac{TP}{TP + FP} \right) \tag{6.12}$$

$$\text{recall} = \left(\frac{TP}{TP + FN} \right) \tag{6.13}$$

The F-score is then calculated with the weighted average of precision and recall:

$$\text{Fscore} = 2 \cdot \left(\frac{\text{precision} \cdot \text{recall}}{\text{precision} + \text{recall}} \right) \tag{6.14}$$

Absolute error: It is measured as the difference between the inferred values for a tuple of records and the actual value. It is given in the following equation:

$$\Delta t = t_0 - t \tag{6.15}$$

RMSe: It is a statistical measure of the size of a varying amount likewise called as the quadratic mean. It can be computed for a progression of discrete values or a persistently varying function. It is given in the following equation:

$$t_{\text{RMS}} = \sqrt{\frac{\sum_{i=1}^{n} t_i^2}{n}} \tag{6.16}$$

For a variant of t over a continuous distribution $P(x)$, RMS is given in the following equation:

$$t_{\text{RMS}} = \sqrt{\frac{\int [p(t)]^2 \, dt}{\int [p(t)] \, dt}} \tag{6.17}$$

6.4.6 CROSS-VALIDATION AND RESULTS OBTAINED

Cross-validation deals with the partition in the initial set of data into k mutual subset. If D is the dataset that deals with the process of data classification, it is segregated into a number of folds such as $D_1, D_2, D_3 \ldots D_k$. The training and testing phases for the entire dataset are performed k number of times. In the first iteration i, the partition D_i is meant for the test dataset, while the remaining separations are used up to train the data model. Hence, during the first iteration in developing the model, the partition $D_1, D_2, D_3 \ldots D_k$ serves to be the training datasets to derive the first data model. During the second iteration, the data partition other that D_2 serves to be the training dataset for the development of the data model over the test on the data partition D_2. The accuracy of the method is then determined in accordance with the total number of correctly classified records.

The dataset used consists of 732 instances of records and 23 attributes involved in the evaluation and development of the model. Out of 23 attributes, Postprandial Plasma Glucose (PPG), Glycosylated Hemoglobin (A1c), Mean Blood Glucose (MBG), and Fasting Plasma Glucose (FPG) are the attributes selected for evaluation. By setting up 10-fold cross-validation, over the number of iterations and generations, the tree obtained by the classifier model is depicted in Figure 6.5. The generated tree provides the root node to be PPG, with a split value of about > 269 and ≤ 269.500

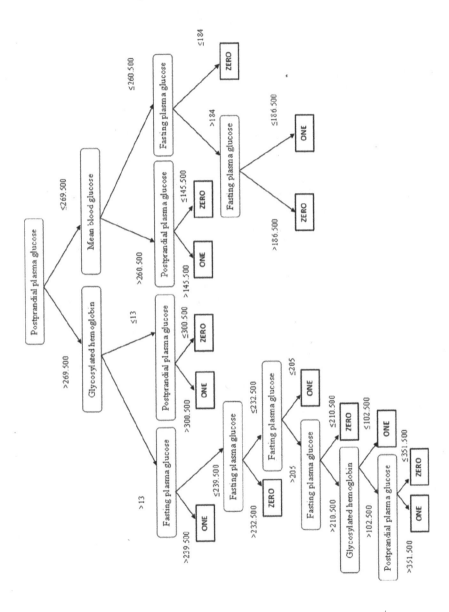

FIGURE 6.5 Generated tree for classification of selected features.

made by A1c and MBG. The split is made with respect to binary segregates of the data tuples. Data discretization among the numeric attribute values involves data partitioning with break points. It represents the split among the class labels with a majority in one side and the remaining part in another. Each set of split value is then determined by the break points with same or different class label values. There are two major cases to be considered for the split value and break point determination:

- During data partition, if the preceding class values are of the same type, then the partition can be merged with that class value.
- During data partition, if the adjacent class consists of the same sort of majority of the similar class label, then they can be merged without breaking the rule. The tree generation process continues until all the branches have been attained with a leaf node, i.e., labeled.

6.5   FORMULATING THE ASSOCIATION AMONG THE RISK FACTORS BY MATHEMATICAL MODEL USING FISHER'S LINEAR DISCRIMINANT ANALYSIS FOR TYPE II DIABETIC PREDICTION

6.5.1   Association of Type II Diabetic Risk with Attribute Measurements

The determined level of accuracy from the set of iterations has been got up to 98.60% with the attributes such as PPG, A1c, MBG, and FPG. The association and correlation among the attributes can be determined by using Karl Pearson correlation coefficient. If the change in one variable affects the change in another variable, then the variables are said to be correlated.

The correlation between the two random variables X and Y is denoted as $r(X,Y)$ and it is defined as follows:

$$r(X,Y) = \frac{\text{Cov}(X,Y)}{\sigma_X \sigma_Y} \qquad (6.18)$$

For the given set of data values (x_i, y_i), $i = 1,2,3\ldots\ldots,n$.
Then,

$$\text{Cov}(X,Y) = E[\{X - E(X)\}\{Y - E(Y)\}] \qquad (6.19)$$

$$\sigma_{X^2} = \frac{1}{n}\sum(x_i - \overline{x})^2 \qquad (6.20)$$

$$\sigma_{Y^2} = \frac{1}{n}\sum(y_i - \overline{y})^2 \qquad (6.21)$$

The limits of correlation among the determined attributes PPG, MBG, FPG, and A1c are given by the following equation:

$$r(X,Y) = \frac{\text{Cov}(X,Y)}{\sigma_X \sigma_Y} = \frac{\frac{1}{n}\sum(x-\bar{x})(y-\bar{y})}{\left[\frac{1}{n}\sum(x-\bar{x})^2 \cdot \frac{1}{n}(y-\bar{y})^2\right]^{1/2}} \qquad (6.22)$$

The set of correlation has been found among (MBG, A1c), (MBG, FPG), (MBG, PPG), and (FPG, PPG) as illustrated in Table 6.5. Hence, Mean Blood Glucose has its strong correlation toward A1c, FPG, and PPG. Similarly, PPG has its strong correlation toward MBG and FPG respectively. With the set of possible combinations, the following combinations among the attribute seem to have a correlated value with its varying discretions. The observed R^2 values among the correlated attributes are 0.5392, 0.5058, 0.4922, and 0.1658, respectively. The comparison among the accuracies with the proposed model PSO-J48 is depicted in Figure 6.6. In Figures 6.7–6.10, exponential curves should meet all the points that lie on them. Meanwhile, curve fitting provides the process of capturing a trend in data by assigning a single function across the entire range. The motto behind curve fitting is to determine the

TABLE 6.5
Determination of Correlation among Attributes

Variables	MBG	A1c	FPG	PPG
MBG	1.000	0.719	0.732	0.733
A1c	0.719	1.000	0.512	0.507
FPG	0.732	0.512	1.000	0.737
PPG	0.733	0.507	0.737	1.000

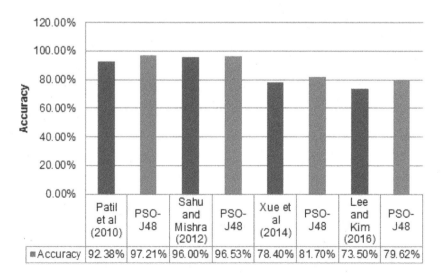

	Patil et al (2010)	PSO-J48	Sahu and Mishra (2012)	PSO-J48	Xue et al (2014)	PSO-J48	Lee and Kim (2016)	PSO-J48
■Accuracy	92.38%	97.21%	96.00%	96.53%	78.40%	81.70%	73.50%	79.62%

FIGURE 6.6 Comparisons among accuraćies with the existing approaches against the proposed model.

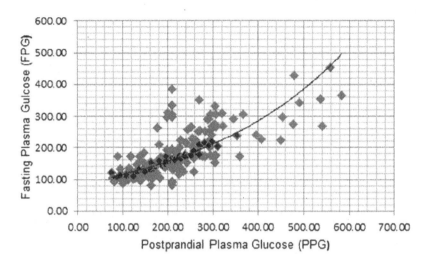

FIGURE 6.7   Observed exponential curve between PPG and FPG with $y = 85.918e0.003x$ and $R^2 = 0.5392$.

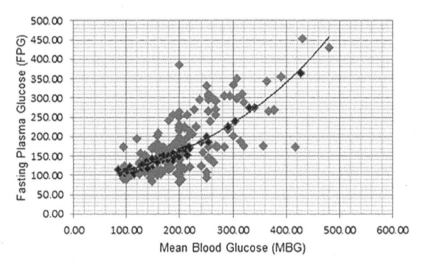

FIGURE 6.8   Observed exponential curve between MBG and FPG with $y = 76.984e0.0037x$ and $R^2 = 0.5058$.

coefficients 'a' and 'b' such that the function fits with the data in an affordable way. The R^2 computation determines the percentage of the response variable and its variation by an exponential model. The more variance encountered by the model, the more closer the data points tend to fit the data model.

6.5.2   COMPARISON OF THE PROPOSED MODEL WITH THE EXISTING APPROACHES

The results obtained using proposed PSO-J48 have been evaluated against various approaches given by authors corresponding to the work of domain. The work has

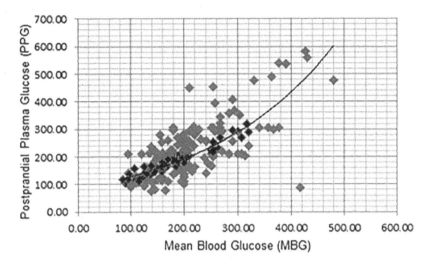

FIGURE 6.9 Observed exponential curve between MBG and PPG with $y = 85.281e0.0041x$ and $R^2 = 0.4927$.

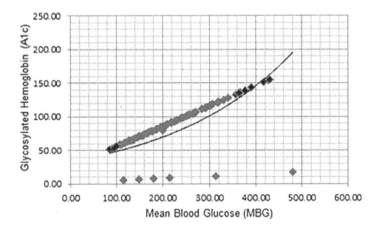

FIGURE 6.10 Observed exponential curve between MBG and PPG with $y = 33.609e0.0037x$ and $R^2 = 0.1658$.

been tested against the dataset used by authors for other such models that they have developed. Table 6.6 provides the experimental results observed in accordance with various other datasets with a comparison to their approaches. Figure 6.6 explains the accuracy of the existing approaches against the proposed model.

Linear discriminant analysis or Fisher's linear discriminant relates to the classification problem, where two or more groups of samples are grouped into clusters of records in which the newer set of observation falls into the known population based upon signified characteristics [20]. The principal component analysis makes over the investigation in a lower dimensional space. Hence, information with maximum

TABLE 6.6

Comparison of the Proposed Model with the Existing Methods for Various Datasets

S.No.	Method	Dataset	Total No. of Features	No. of Features selected	Accuracy (%)
1	Xue et al. (2014)	Lung UCI	56	6	78.40
	Proposed model PSO-J48	dataset		5	81.70
2	Patil et al. (2010)	Pima Indian Diabetic	5	3	92.38
	Proposed model PSO-J48	Dataset		3	97.21
3	Lee and Kim (2016)	Type II Diabetic Data set	15	3	73.50
	Proposed model PSO-J48			3	79.62
4	Sahu and Mishra (2012)	Benchmark colon cancer	2000	5	96.00
	Proposed model PSO-J48	dataset		4	96.53

variances is not suitable for classification problem. The discrimination among the data into different sets of classes will not be made by principal component analysis, and therefore, the linear discriminant analysis has been chosen for data evaluation 21].

Consider the set of d-dimensional samples of $x_1, x_2, x_3 \ldots x_n$; let n_1, n_2 corresponds to the subset of records from D_1, D_2 with ω_1 and ω_2 as labels respectively. The linear combination of components corresponding to x for y is given as $y = w^t x$. With the selected set of features, the formulation among the best separation of classes for MBG, PPG, FPG, and A1c has to be determined. The separation of classes for the attributes has to be suited in the best direction corresponding to w [22]. The mean for 732 subjects in its dimensional space is given in the following equation:

$$m_i = \frac{1}{n_i} \sum_{x \in D_i} x \tag{6.23}$$

For the set of subjects, the sample mean of projected points is given in the following equation:

$$\overline{m_i} = \frac{1}{n_i} \sum_{y \in y_i} y = \frac{1}{n_i} \sum_{x \in D_i} w^t x = w^t m_i \tag{6.24}$$

The separation between the anticipated methods for the two classes zero and one is ascertained by utilizing the following equation:

$$|\overline{m_1} - \overline{m_2}| = |w^t(m_1 - m_2)| \qquad (6.25)$$

The defined scatter for the projected variance is for the pooled data which is given as follows:

$$\left(\frac{1}{n}\left(\overline{s_1}^2 + \overline{s_2}^2\right)\right)$$

Table 6.7 defines the projected pooled data value for the best separation of records among the classes.

The following step is to locate the linear function $w^t x$ in which

$$J(w) = \frac{|\overline{m_1} - \overline{m_2}|^2}{\left(\overline{s_1}^2 + \overline{s_2}^2\right)} \qquad (6.26)$$

This ought to be considered to be higher and independent of $\|w\|$. The within-class scatter matrix can be determined using $S_w = S_1 + S_2$ and the between-class matrix is found using $S_B = (m_1 - m_2)(m_1 - m_2)^t$. The observed class covariance matrix is given in Tables 6.8 and 6.9.

The within-class scatter matrix is proportional to the sample covariance for the pooled dimensional data. For S_B and S_W, the function is given as $J(w) = \frac{w^t S_B w}{w^t S_w w}$. Hence, the vector w that maximizes to formulate the condition should satisfy $S_B w = \lambda S_W w$, which implies the formulation of $S_W^{-1} S_B w = \lambda w$, which again denotes Eigen Equation. Hence, we have obtained the value of Fisher's discriminant analysis

TABLE 6.7
Measured Pooled Within-Class Covariance Matrix

	MBG	A1c	FPG	PPG
MBG	3592.459	984.691	2091.529	2694.772
A1c	984.691	668.195	524.821	662.446
FPG	2091.529	524.821	3397.268	2605.972
PPG	2694.772	662.446	2605.972	5604.501

TABLE 6.8
Measured Within-Class Covariance Matrix for Class 0

	MBG	A1c	FPG	PPG
MBG	2434.727	722.569	923.531	1330.803
A1c	722.569	546.624	175.152	283.505
FPG	923.531	175.152	1914.389	1544.411
PPG	1330.803	283.505	1544.411	2984.082

TABLE 6.9

Measured Within-Class Covariance Matrix for Class 1

	MBG	A1c	FPG	PPG
MBG	5655.680	1451.827	4173.043	5125.532
A1c	1451.827	884.850	1147.975	1337.765
FPG	4173.043	1147.975	6039.942	4497.804
PPG	5125.532	1337.765	4497.804	10274.409

which provides the ratio of between-class scatter to within-class scatter and proves to be different [23].

6.5.3 TEST INTERPRETATION

The esteem of elucidation can be decided by the hypothesis test. Let H_0 be the within-class covariance matrix to be assumed as in equal state and H_1 be the within-class covariance matrix in a different state, with H_0 being the null hypothesis and H_1 being the alternate hypothesis.

From the results, it is observed that the p-value is lower than that of the level of alpha which is 0.05. So, we can reject the null hypothesis H_0 and accept the alternate hypothesis H_1. Therefore, it has been concluded from the mathematical model that the within-class covariance matrices are different. The state of risk is to reject the null hypothesis while it is true by lower than 0.01%. Table 6.10 provides the results observed with Fisher's discriminant analysis using observed and critical values.

The goodness of fit computed over χ^2 analysis among the observed and the expected frequencies of (A_i, B_j) is computed using the following equation:

$$\chi^2 = \sum_{i=1}^{C} \sum_{j=1}^{R} \left(O_{ij} - E_{ij}\right)^2 / E_{ij} \tag{6.27}$$

The χ^2 statistic tests the hypothesis that H_0 and H_1 are independent. The test is based upon significance level of $(r-1) * (c-1)$ degrees of freedom. The computed degrees of freedom for the statistical test is 10, and for 10 degrees of freedom, the probability

TABLE 6.10

Fisher's F Asymptotic Approximation

F (Observed value)	22.519
F (Critical value)	65326.551
DF1	10
DF2	651387
P-value	<0.0001
α	0.05

is observed to be 18.30 with the observed $\chi^2 = 225.19$ respectively. Since our value is more prominent than that of the probabilistic value $P < 0.0001$, we can reject the null hypothesis and conclude that the attributes PPG, MBG, FPG, and A1c are dependent on each other.

6.5.4 TEST EVALUATION

The test evaluation has been done using ROC which provides a medium for sensitivity and specificity report. The points in the curve determine the set of sensitivity/specificity pairs that correspond to the decision threshold value. The area provided by the curve provides the mechanism of distinguishing among the signified class labels which reveal diseased and normal conditions. The discrimination is determined for every possible cutoff criterion in which some of the cases with the disease are to be correctly classified (True Positive) and some of the cases are correctly classified for those without the disease (True Negative). But there will be cases where individuals with the disease will be wrongly classified as negative and those without the disease will be classified as positive. Table 6.11 provides the best separation for the confusion matrix in classifying the data for the population with and without the disease.

The statistics corresponding to sensitivity and specificity is given in the following equations:

$$positive\_likelihood\_ratio = \frac{Sensitivity}{1 - specificity} \tag{6.28}$$

$$negative\_likelihood\_ratio = \frac{1 - Sensitivity}{Specificity} \tag{6.29}$$

Sensitivity defines the state as the estimate of the probability that signifies the test result as positive if the disease is present (percentage of TP). Specificity defines the state as negative if the probability that signifies the test result is not present (percentage of TN).

6.5.5 ROC ANALYSIS

The efficacy of the method has been tested for ROC analysis in which the cumulative distribution function signifies the value of ∞ to the specified threshold value. The curve provides the estimate in accordance with probability detection in the y-axis and the cumulative distribution function in the x-axis. The class distribution

TABLE 6.11
Testing Criteria

Test Criteria	Disease Status	
Positive cases	True Positive (TP)	False Positive (FP)
Negative cases	False Negative (FN)	True Negative (TN)

in accordance with the binary classification problem has been evaluated for analysis. Meanwhile, the possible way of determining optimal modes can be taken into consideration for the experimental analysis [24]. The ROC curve in Figure 6.11 signifies the plot for sensitivity and specificity for different cutoff points [25]. A decision threshold value is used by each point that represents the pair of data. The perfect test interpretation and discrimination have been interpreted if there is no form of overlap among the distributions. Table 6.12 provides the results obtained using ROC.

Hence, from the observed results, the AUC equals to 0.887, which is nearer to the value 1. Therefore, among the two sets of distribution, there are no overlaps and the values of sensitivity and specificity pairs in which the ROC of the curve lies at the upper left corner corresponding to the plot as in Figure 6.11. As a result, the distribution concerning the cumulative function and the probability estimate values indicate that there exist no controversies among the class distribution. The probability of detection is also near to the optimal value of 1. Therefore, for the considered dataset, the perceived model performs well in terms of accuracy, sensitivity, and specificity also with the model [26].

The proposed model using PSO-J48 algorithm provides an insight into the observed data, which corresponds to the region of Theni. Nature, habits, locality, likelihood, and dietary conditions of the people may vary from region to region. Each group of people may adhere to policies and framework in which the obsolete way of living can vary from time to time. The objective of this research work is to develop a predictive model for type II diabetic risk prediction using PSO and decision tree algorithm. The developed model best spots the risk factors that are more predominant to have a strong correlation with the observed data. Medical practitioners can well utilize the developed method to observe the predominant risk factor that corresponds to the specified disease. Also, the model can well be adhered to in

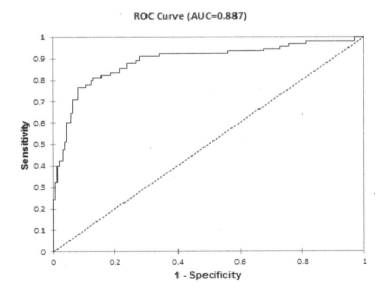

FIGURE 6.11   ROC for sensitivity vs. specificity.

TABLE 6.12
ROC Analysis Report

Area Under the Curve (AUC)	0.887
Standard Error	0.0281
Sensitivity	98.66
Significance level P (area = 0.5)	<0.0001

practice for the determination of correlation patterns that exist between the risk factors and its test case criterion concerning Accuracy, Sensitivity, Specificity, and its P-value [27].

From the analysis report, it has been observed that the attributes MBG, PPG, FPG, and A1c have a resilient dependency among them regarding test measures, test interpretation, and evaluation.

6.6 PERFORMANCE OF THE PROPOSED APPROACHES FOR REAL-WORLD DATASETS

This research has presented three different predictive models for evaluating the risk factors related to medical data. Each of the models has its own set of parametric values with regard to the total number of features selected. The fitness function evaluation for all the models has been made using J48 (Java execution of C4.5 Decision Tree algorithm). The features selected by ACO-DT model vary significantly when compared to the other two models. Table 6.13 summarizes the features selected by the proposed approaches.

With the selected set of features from the three models, the model corresponding to BHS-DT and PSO-DT found to have MBG, PPG, and A1c in common. But the model corresponding to ACO-DT has only one feature FPG in common to the PSO-DT model. The interpretation with expert evaluation concluded that the features selected by the model PSO-DT seem to be more efficient and well correlated than that of the other two models. Also, the accuracy of the PSO-DT model is found to be higher when compared to the other two models in terms of prediction. Figure 6.12 provides a comparison in predictive accuracy obtained by the models.

Similarly, the analysis report has been evaluated for heart disease dataset by utilizing all the three models. Among the three models, PSO-DT is found to be more efficient in terms of accuracy and the number of features selected by the model. ACO-DT selected 16 features, BHS-DT with 8 features, and PSO-DT with 6 features that correspond to heart disease. Figure 6.13 provides the comparison of the models in terms of accuracy value obtained.

Since the dataset has been collected across a specified region corresponding to rural area, the outcome is shown in terms of majorly influencing risk factors and its correlation. This will help the medical experts to work out with regard to the relationship among the risk factors in accordance with their varying levels. As an outcome, risk factors such as MBG, PPG, A1c, and FPG have more correlation effect among each other than the other attributes.

TABLE 6.13

Features Selected by the Proposed Models for Type II Diabetic Data

S. No.	Proposed Model	Features Selected
1	ACO-DT	FPG, Total Cholesterol, BU, SGPT, NHDL, SGOT, GGT, Albumin, Globulin, Total Protein, and HDL
2	BHS-DT	PPG, A1c, and MBG
3	PSO-DT	MBG, PPG, A1c, and FPG

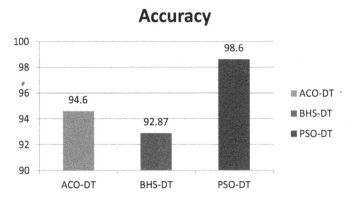

FIGURE 6.12   Comparison among the proposed approaches in accuracy for type II diabetic data.

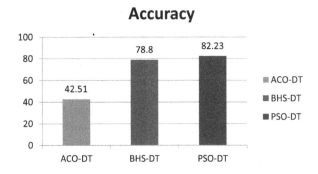

FIGURE 6.13   Comparison among the proposed approaches in accuracy for heart disease data.

6.6.1 SUMMARY

Data classification and optimization in prediction play a significant role in medical data analysis. Collecting and processing medical data with its range values seems to be a challenging problem. The entire formulation of the research work signifies the development of a decision support model with an improved PSO and decision tree algorithm. The improvement is made in fixing the operating parameter, i.e., modified self-adaptive inertial weight with convergence logic for the particles to explore in the given search space to find a near-optimal solution. The dataset of 732 records with 23 attributes, including the class label, has been used for analysis. The test result demonstrates that the proposed method produces four important risk factors with improved accuracy of about 98.60%. The effectiveness of the proposed model has been validated against data, and the methodology is given by various authors. Meanwhile, the association among the selected features such as MBG, PPG, A1c, and FPG has been determined. A strong correlation has been observed for MBG with A1c. Also, FPG and PPG have strong correlation with MBG and FPG respectively. The observed R^2 values among the correlated attributes are 0.5392, 0.5058, 0.4927, and 0.1658, which are also found to be significant.

A mathematical model has been developed using Fisher's LDA for the discovered attributes. The within-class covariance matrix for class zero and one has been calculated, and the test interpretation results prove that the value $\chi^2 = 222.19$ is significantly greater than the probabilistically observed value $P < 0.0001$. Therefore, the alternate hypothesis is accepted for the signified F value across the probabilistic measure in degrees of freedom. The test interpretation with ROC analysis value has been observed as 0.887 with a significant level of <0.0001. Hence, for the data corresponding to type II diabetes of 732 subjects, the risk prevalence has been found across MBG, PPG, A1c, and FPG. The developed model can be used by physicians for earlier determination of the disease and to reduce clinical test, which in addition reduces the cost of treatment. The proof for the deployment of the model is enclosed in Appendix IV. Also, it has been suggested by the medical experts that the proposed model can be deployed in other regions for predicting the risk factors related to NCD.

REFERENCES

1. Leslie R.D.G., Kilpatrick E.S. (2009). Translating the A1C Assay Into Estimated Average Glucose Values. *Diabetes Care* [Internet]. 2009 Jan 1; 32(1), e11–e11. doi:10.2337/dc08-1524
2. Morris F. Collen. (1994). The Origins of Informatics. *Journal of the American Medical Informatics Association*, 1(2), 91–107. doi:10.1136/JAMIA.1994.95236152
3. H. R. Hapsara. (2005). World Health Organization (WHO): Global Health Situation. *Encyclopedia of Statistical Sciences* [Internet]. 2005 Dec 1; 1–8. doi:10.1002/0471667196. ess7232
4. Laura E. Allen. (2013). Defining Private Property Interests in America's New Economic Reality: The Case for the Primacy of Federal Law in Takings Litigation. *Journal of Law and Commerce*, 31, 221–254. doi:10.5195/JLC.2013.52

5. Jacques Teghem. (2010). Metaheuristics. From Design to Implementation, El-Ghazali Talbi. John Wiley & Sons Inc. (2009). XXI + 593 pp., Publication 978-0-470-27858-1. *European Journal of Operational Research*, 205(2), 486–487. doi:10.1016/J.EJOR.2009.12.010

6. U. Aickelin. (2005). Handbook of Metaheuristics (International Series in Operations Research and Management Science). *Journal of the Operational Research Society*, 56(5), 614.

7. James Kennedy, Russell C. Eberhart. (2002). Particle Swarm Optimization. *Proceedings of the IEEE International Conference on Neural Networks*, 4, 1942–1948. doi:10.1109/ICNN.1995.488968

8. Rehab F. Abdel-Kader. (2010). Genetically Improved PSO Algorithm for Efficient Data Clustering. *2010 Second International Conference on Machine Learning and Computing* [Internet]. 2010; doi:10.1109/icmlc.2010.19

9. Imad Zyout, Joanna Czajkowska, Marcin Grzegorzek. (2015). Multi-Scale Textural Feature Extraction and Particle Swarm Optimization Based Model Selection for False Positive Reduction in Mammography. *Computerized Medical Imaging and Graphics*, 46, 95–107. doi:10.1016/J.COMPMEDIMAG.2015.02.005

10. Russell C. Eberhart, Yuhui Shi. (2001). Tracking and Optimizing Dynamic Systems With Particle Swarms. *Proceedings of the 2001 Congress on Evolutionary Computation*, 1, 94–100. doi:10.1109/CEC.2001.934376

11. Li-Yeh Chuang, Sheng-Wei Tsai, Cheng-Hong Yang. (2011). Improved Binary Particle Swarm Optimization Using Catfish Effect for Feature Selection. *Expert Systems With Applications*, 38(10), 12699–12707. doi:10.1016/J.ESWA.2011.04.057

12. Vinod C. Kaggal, Ravikumar Komandur Elayavilli, Saeed Mehrabi, Joshua J. Pankratz, Sunghwan Sohn, Yanshan Wang, Dingcheng Li, Majid Mojarad Rastegar, Sean P. Murphy, Jason L. Ross, Rajeev Chaudhry, James D. Buntrock, Hongfang Liu. (2016). Toward a Learning Health-care System - Knowledge Delivery at the Point of Care Empowered by Big Data and NLP. *Biomedical Informatics Insights*, 8(Suppl 1), 13–22. doi:10.4137/BII.S37977

13. A. SheikAbdullah. (2012). A Data Mining Model to Predict and Analyze the Events Related to Coronary Heart Disease Using Decision Trees With Particle Swarm Optimization for Feature Selection. *International Journal of Computer Applications*, 55(8), 49–55. doi:10.5120/8779-2736

14. A. Sheik Abdullah, S. Selvakumar, P. Karthikeyan, M. Venkatesh. (2017). Comparing the Efficacy of Decision Tree and its Variants using Medical Data. *Indian Journal of Science and Technology*, 10(18), 1–8. doi:10.17485/IJST/2017/V10I18/111768

15. James Kennedy, Russell C. Eberhart. (2002). Particle Swarm Optimization. *Proceedings of the IEEE International Conference on Neural Networks*, 4, 1942–1948. doi:10.1109/ICNN.1995.488968

16. José García-Nieto, Enrique Alba. (2011). Restart Particle Swarm Optimization with Velocity Modulation: A Scalability Test. *Soft Computing*, 15(11), 2221–2232. doi:10.1007/S00500-010-0648-1

17. Yuhui Shi, Russell C. Eberhart. (1998). A modified particle swarm optimizer. 1998 IEEE *International Conference on Evolutionary Computation Proceedings IEEE World Congress on Computational Intelligence (Cat No98TH8360)* [Internet]. doi:10.1109/icec.1998.699146

18. Amin Ebrahim Sorkhabi, Mehran Deljavan Amiri, Alireza Khanteymoori. (2017). Duality Evolution: An Efficient Approach to Constraint Handling in Multi-Objective Particle Swarm Optimization. *Soft Computing*, 21(24), 7251–7267. doi:10.1007/S00500-016-2422-5

19. Pierre Baldi, Søren Brunak, Yves Chauvin, Claus A. Andersen, Henrik Nielsen. (2000). Assessing the Accuracy of Prediction Algorithms for Classification: An Overview. *Bioinformatics*, 16(5), 412–424. doi:10.1093/BIOINFORMATICS/16.5.412

20. R. A. Fisher. (1936). The Use of Multiple Measurements in Taxonomic Problems. *Annals of Human Genetics*, 7(2), 179–188. doi:10.1111/J.1469-1809.1936.TB02137.X

21. R. A. Fisher. (1938). The Statistical Utilization of Multiple Measurements. Annals of Human Genetics, 8(4), 376–386. doi:10.1111/J.1469-1809.1938.TB02189.X

22. Nello Cristianini. (2014). Fisher Discriminant Analysis (Linear Discriminant Analysis). *Dictionary of Bioinformatics and Computational Biology* [Internet]. 2004 Oct 15; doi:10.1002/0471650129.dob0238

23. Friday Zinzendoff Okwonu, Abdul Rahim Othman, Pulau Pinang. (2012). A Model Classification Technique for Linear Discriminant Analysis for Two Groups. *International Journal of Computer Science Issues*, 9(3), 213–220.

24. Matthias Greiner, Dirk U. Pfeiffer, Ronald D. Smith. (2000). Principles and Practical Application of the Receiver-Operating Characteristic Analysis for Diagnostic Tests. *Preventive Veterinary Medicine*, 45(1), 23–41. doi:10.1016/S0167-5877(00)00115-X

25. Elizabeth R. DeLong, David M. DeLong, Daniel L. Clarke-Pearson. (1988). Comparing the Areas Under Two or More Correlated Receiver Operating Characteristic Curves: A Nonparametric Approach. *Biometrics*, 44(3), 837–845. doi:10.2307/2531595

26. Ian A. Gardner, Matthias Greiner. (2006). Receiver-Operating Characteristic Curves and Likelihood Ratios: Improvements over Traditional Methods for the Evaluation and Application of Veterinary Clinical Pathology Tests. *Veterinary Clinical Pathology*, 35(1), 8–17. doi:10.1111/J.1939-165X.2006.TB00082.X

27. Ronald D. Smith, Barrett D. Slenning. (2000). Decision Analysis: Dealing with Uncertainty in Diagnostic Testing. *Preventive Veterinary Medicine*, 45(1), 139–162. doi:10.1016/S0167-5877(00)00121-5

7 Case-Based Analysis in Medical Informatics

7.1 DIABETIC PRIMARY

CASE STUDY REPORT

Diabetes is a chronic condition that inhibits the body's ability to regulate blood glucose levels. There are two forms of diabetes: type 1 and type 2. With type 1 diabetes, the body's immune system mistakenly attacks insulin-producing cells in the pancreas, resulting in an insulin deficiency. Type 2 diabetes, on the other hand, is caused by a mix of hereditary and environmental factors that cause the body to become insulin resistant. Diabetes is normally diagnosed using a combination of diagnostic testing, a medical history review, and a physical examination. Diagnostic tests include the fasting blood glucose test, the oral glucose tolerance test, the glycated hemoglobin (HbA1c) test, and the random blood glucose test. These tests aid in determining whether a person has diabetes and, if so, what type.

A medical history review and physical examination, in addition to diagnostic tests, are critical components of primary diabetes analysis. Questions about the individual's symptoms, family history of diabetes, and any other pertinent medical issues will be asked during the medical history review [1]. The physical examination will include determining the individual's weight, blood pressure, and overall health, as well as looking for indicators of diabetic complications. Once diabetes has been diagnosed, the primary analysis will include formulating a treatment plan. Generally, diabetes is treated with a mix of lifestyle modifications (such as diet and exercise) and medication (such as insulin or oral medications). Frequent blood sugar monitoring is also essential in treating diabetes and preventing complications.

Type 2 diabetes mellitus is a metabolic condition characterized by elevated blood glucose levels caused by insulin resistance or inadequate insulin production. Epidemiology and aetiology of type 2 diabetes are influenced by numerous factors.

7.1.1 Challenges Faced in Type II Diabetes

Type 2 diabetes can bring a number of difficulties for those who have been diagnosed with it. Among them, the major challenges are:

- Managing blood sugar levels: Keeping blood sugar levels under control is one of the most difficult problems for people with diabetes type 2. This usually entails frequently monitoring blood sugar levels, making dietary modifications, and maybe taking medicine or insulin to control blood sugar levels.

DOI: 10.1201/9781003330189-7

- Adhering to a healthy lifestyle: Maintaining a healthy lifestyle is vital for treating type 2 diabetes, although it can be difficult for certain people. Making dietary adjustments, increasing physical exercise, stopping smoking, and managing stress are a few examples.
- Prevention complications: Cardiovascular disease, nerve damage, kidney damage, eye damage, and foot damage are more prevalent in those with type 2 diabetes. Often, preventing these problems entails regular monitoring of blood sugar levels, management of underlying health concerns, and living a healthy lifestyle.
- Dealing with the emotional impact: A diagnosis of type 2 diabetes can be emotionally taxing, and many people may experience anxiety, despair, or tension [1]. It is critical to address these mental issues and get help when necessary.
- Medication and treatment management: Many people with type 2 diabetes require many drugs or treatments to control their illness, which can be difficult to track and manage. To ensure that medications and treatments are used efficiently and safely, it is critical to collaborate closely with healthcare practitioners.

Overall, managing type 2 diabetes is a difficult and continuing process that necessitates close monitoring and management. Many people with type 2 diabetes, however, may successfully manage their illness and live healthy, fulfilling lives with the right treatment and support.

7.1.2 Epidemiology

Type 2 diabetes mellitus (T2DM) is a metabolic disease characterized by high blood glucose levels due to insulin resistance and inadequate insulin synthesis. According to the International Diabetes Federation (IDF), about 537 million adults (20–79 years) would have diabetes in 2021, with 90% of them having type 2 diabetes. There were over 463 million instances of type 2 diabetes [2] globally in 2019. According to statistical projections [3] derived from a model incorporating data from 1990 to 2017, the global prevalence of diabetes could increase to 7,079 per 100,000 by 2030 and 7,862 by 2040. The top and lower confidence limits for this projection for 2040 are 9,904 and 5,821 per 100,000. The prevalence is rising, and it is predicted that 700 million people worldwide will have diabetes by the year 2045. In low- and middle-income nations, type 2 diabetes is most prevalent.

Type 2 diabetes is a complex condition with a number of risk factors. The following are some typical risk factors [4]:

- Obesity and a sedentary lifestyle: Obesity and a sedentary lifestyle are important risk factors for type 2 diabetes.
- Age: When people get older, risk of having type 2 diabetes rises.
- Family history: People who have diabetes in their family are more likely to get it themselves.

- Racial and ethnic background: Some racial and ethnic groups, such as African Americans, Hispanic Americans, Native Americans, and Asians, are more susceptible to developing type 2 diabetes.
- Women who have experienced gestational diabetes have a higher risk of developing Type 2 diabetes later in life.

The following is a breakdown of T2DM epidemiology [3] by region:

1. North America: Diabetes affects approximately 34.2 million people (10.5% of the population) in the United States, with 90%–95% of them having T2DM. Diabetes affects approximately 11 million Canadians, with 90%–95% having type 2 diabetes.
2. South America: The frequency of T2DM varies by country in South America. In Brazil, for example, roughly 17.7 million people have diabetes, with 90%–95% having T2DM.
3. Europe: The prevalence of T2DM varies by country in Europe. In Germany, for example, roughly 7 million people have diabetes, with 90%–95% having T2DM.
4. Asia: The incidence of type 2 diabetes is significant in Asia. According to the IDF, around 191 million Chinese individuals have diabetes, with 90%–95% having T2DM. In India, around 77 million people have diabetes, with 90%–95% having type 2 diabetes.
5. Africa: The frequency of T2DM is quickly growing in Africa. According to the IDF, around 19.4 million Nigerians have diabetes, with 90%–95% having type 2 diabetes.

7.1.3 Aetiology

Type 2 diabetes has a complex aetiology that is caused by a complex interaction of hereditary and environmental factors:

- Genetics: Type 2 diabetes develops largely as a result of genetic factors. An increased risk of type 2 diabetes has been linked to specific gene variants.
- Insulin resistance: Type 2 diabetes is characterized by insulin resistance. When there is insulin resistance, the body's cells are less receptive to the hormone, which raises blood sugar levels.
- Pancreatic beta-cell dysfunction: Together with insulin resistance, pancreatic beta cells' decreased insulin secretion is a risk factor for type 2 diabetes.
- Environmental variables: Lifestyle factors such as diet, exercise, and weight can have a significant impact on the development of type 2 diabetes. A higher risk of type 2 diabetes is associated with diets high in saturated and trans fats and low in fiber, fruits, and vegetables. The benefits of physical activity include improved insulin sensitivity and a reduced risk of type 2 diabetes. Obesity contributes significantly to the development of type 2 diabetes and is associated with insulin resistance and reduced beta-cell function in the pancreas.

Type 2 diabetes has a complex epidemiology and aetiology that is influenced by a number of variables, including genetics, lifestyle, and environmental factors.

7.1.4 MAKING THE DIAGNOSIS

Here are some of the common symptoms [5] associated with T2DM:

- Frequent urination: Increased blood sugar levels cause the kidneys to work harder, leading to frequent urination.
- Excessive thirst: As the body loses more fluids through frequent urination, it triggers the thirst mechanism, leading to excessive thirst.
- Fatigue: T2DM can cause fatigue due to the body's inability to utilize glucose for energy properly.
- Blurred vision: High amounts of blood sugar can cause the lens of the eye to expand, resulting in impaired vision.
- Slow healing of wounds: T2DM can slow down the healing process of wounds due to poor circulation and high blood sugar levels.
- Numbness or tingling in the hands or feet: High blood sugar levels can cause numbness or tingling in the hands or feet due to nerve damage.
- Unexplained weight loss: Some people with T2DM may experience unexplained weight loss due to the body's inability to utilize glucose properly for energy.
- Increased hunger: The body may crave more food than usual, even after eating, as it struggles to utilize glucose properly.

If a person experience any of these symptoms, it is essential to consult a healthcare professional for proper diagnosis and treatment.

7.1.5 PROGNOSIS

The prognosis for type 2 diabetes varies based on a number of factors, including age, lifestyle, medical history, and the presence of other diseases. Type 2 diabetes is a chronic condition that cannot be cured but can be managed with the right treatment and lifestyle modifications.

If left untreated or poorly controlled, it can result in cardiovascular disease, nerve damage, kidney damage, eye damage, and foot injury. These issues can have a significant impact on quality of life and are potentially fatal.

1. Obesity: Obesity is a substantial risk factor for developing T2DM, and it can also affect the disease's prognosis. While examining the prognostic factors in T2DM, obesity is one of the important factors that can influence the disease's course and therapy. Obesity is linked to insulin resistance, which is a defining feature of T2DM. This resistance causes cells to have poor glucose uptake and utilization, resulting in increased blood glucose levels. This in turn increases the risk of diabetes complications such as cardiovascular disease, neuropathy, nephropathy, and retinopathy.

Obesity has been linked to an increased chance of acquiring T2DM, as well as a worse prognosis once the condition has been diagnosed, according to several studies [6]. Obesity people with T2DM have higher HbA1c values, indicating poorer blood glucose management, as well as higher fasting plasma glucose levels. Obesity can also make managing T2DM through lifestyle changes more challenging, as it frequently necessitates more aggressive treatment techniques such as medication and insulin therapy. Furthermore, obesity can make it more difficult to treat other comorbidities associated with T2DM, such as hypertension and dyslipidemia [6]. It is a significant prognostic factor in T2DM and should be considered when formulating treatment strategies for individuals with the illness. Obesity can be effectively managed through lifestyle modifications, weight loss, and other therapies, which can improve glycemic control and lower the risk of complications associated with T2DM.

2. Cardiovascular disease: Cardiovascular disease (CVD) is the greatest cause of death among people with T2DM and a prominent consequence of the condition [6]. Those with T2DM have a higher risk of having CVD than people without diabetes. Many variables contribute to this elevated risk, including insulin resistance, hypertension, and chronic inflammation.

Insulin resistance, a hallmark of T2DM, can result in endothelial dysfunction, a condition in which the blood vessel lining becomes damaged. This damage can contribute to the development of atherosclerosis, a condition in which plaques form inside the arteries, resulting in decreased blood flow to essential organs such as the heart and brain. Dyslipidemia, or faulty lipid metabolism, is also common in persons with T2DM and can contribute to atherosclerosis progression. Another common complication of T2DM is hypertension, which can further damage blood vessels and raise the risk of CVD. Chronic inflammation is another prevalent hallmark of T2DM, and it has been linked to the development and progression of atherosclerosis.

3. Nerve damage: Neuropathy, a common complication of T2DM, can affect nerves throughout the body. Individuals with poorly controlled blood sugar, hypertension, and cholesterol levels are more susceptible to develop neuropathy. Neuropathy can cause numbness, tingling, burning, and pain in the feet and hands, among other symptoms. It can also have an impact on the digestive system, causing constipation, diarrhea, and gastroparesis, a disease in which the stomach takes an abnormally long time to empty its contents.

4. Kidney damage: Nephropathy, also known as kidney damage, is a frequent complication of T2DM, and it can proceed to chronic kidney disease (CKD) and end-stage renal disease (ESRD). Those with poorly managed blood sugar levels, high blood pressure, and dyslipidemia are more likely to develop nephropathy [7]. Proteinuria, or the presence of protein in the urine, and decreased kidney function are two indicators of nephropathy. It can eventually lead to renal failure and the need for dialysis or a kidney transplant.

5. Eye damage: Diabetic Retinopathy is a typical complication of type 2 diabetes that develops when high blood sugar levels damage the retinal blood vessels [7] (the light-sensitive layer at the back of your eye). This can lead to vision issues like fuzzy vision, dark patches, and difficulties seeing at night. T2D can also raise your risk of developing cataracts, which are hazy regions in your eye's lens. This can result in hazy vision and difficulty seeing in bright light. T2D increases your risk of developing glaucoma, a disorder that destroys the visual nerve and can lead to blindness if left untreated.

6. Foot damages: Diabetic neuropathy is caused by high blood sugar levels, which can damage the nerves in your foot. This might cause numbness, tingling, or discomfort in your feet and legs, making injuries or infections harder to detect. Diabetes neuropathy can also result in foot ulcers, which are open sores or wounds that do not heal adequately. These ulcers can get infected, requiring amputation in severe cases.

7. Impaired circulation: T2D can also impair blood circulation to your feet, causing foot pain and making wound healing more difficult.

However, with good medication and control, people with type 2 diabetes can typically live long, healthy lives without developing serious complications. Maintaining healthy blood sugar levels is normally accomplished through diet, exercise, and medication as prescribed by a healthcare expert, as well as regular monitoring of blood sugar levels and other health markers.

7.1.6 Factors to be Considered for Blood Test

Blood testing is important in the diagnosis and management of T2DM. Many blood tests are available for assessing blood sugar management, detecting problems, and monitoring treatment.

Fasting plasma glucose testing is the most common blood test used to identify T2DM. This test detects the amount of glucose in the blood after a fasting period of 12 hours. Diabetes is indicated by a fasting plasma glucose level of 126 mg/dL or above on two different occasions.

The oral glucose tolerance test is also used to identify T2DM. Two hours after consuming a sugary beverage, the blood glucose level will be measured. A blood glucose concentration of 200 mg/dL or greater indicates diabetes. Many blood tests are widely used to evaluate diabetic patients' conditions and determine their risk of complications [8]. Normal values for these tests can vary based on the individual and their specific circumstances; however, here are some broad guidelines:

- Fasting blood glucose: A diabetic's fasting blood glucose level should be between 70 and 130 mg/dL (3.9 and 7.2 mmol/L). However, depending on your specific circumstances, your healthcare professional may establish alternative goal ranges.
- Hemoglobin A1c (HbA1c) tests the average blood sugar levels during the previous 2–3 months. A normal HbA1c result for someone with diabetes is less than 7%; however, your healthcare practitioner may set alternative target ranges based on your specific needs.

- Lipid profile: This test evaluates cholesterol and triglyceride levels in the blood, which might be useful in determining cardiovascular risk. According to the American Diabetes Association, patients with diabetes should aim for LDL cholesterol levels below 100 mg/dL (2.6 mmol/L), HDL cholesterol levels over 40 mg/dL (1.0 mmol/L) for men and 50 mg/dL (1.3 mmol/L) for women, and triglyceride levels below 150 mg/dL (1.7 mmol/L).
- Blood tests can also be used to detect complications of T2DM, such as kidney damage and high cholesterol levels. The blood test for kidney function is called serum creatinine, which measures the level of creatinine in the blood. The blood test for cholesterol levels is called a lipid profile, which measures the levels of total cholesterol, LDL cholesterol, HDL cholesterol, and triglycerides.

It is critical to remember that these are only guidelines. Further goal ranges may be established by the healthcare practitioner depending on unique circumstances and medical history. Working closely with the healthcare team to monitor blood sugar levels and other health markers over time can also help prevent problems and improve diabetes management.

7.1.7 Medications Available for T2DM

Individuals with type 2 diabetes either do not make enough insulin or do not use insulin adequately, resulting in high blood sugar levels. To assist manage type 2 diabetes, various drugs are available, and treatment strategies are frequently individualized depending on individual needs and medical history as suggested by several studies [2].

- Typically, metformin is the initial treatment for type 2 diabetes. Metformin is an orally administered medication that reduces the amount of glucose produced by the liver and increases insulin sensitivity. It is frequently used in conjunction with other drugs to assist lower blood sugar levels, such as sulfonylureas or insulin.
- Another type of drug often used to treat type 2 diabetes is sulfonylureas. These drugs cause the pancreas to generate more insulin. Glipizide, glyburide, and glimepiride are examples of sulfonylureas [9]. These drugs can help lower blood sugar levels, but there is a risk of hypoglycemia (low blood sugar).
- DPP-4 inhibitors are a newer class of drug that works by inhibiting DPP-4, an enzyme that breaks down hormones that promote insulin production. These drugs can help reduce blood sugar levels and have a minimal risk of inducing hypoglycemia. Sitagliptin, saxagliptin, and linagliptin are examples of DPP-4 inhibitors [9].
- Glucagon-like peptide 1 (GLP-1) receptor agonists are a second class of drugs used to treat type 2 diabetes. These medications mimic the properties of the hormone GLP-1, which boosts insulin production and reduces appetite. GLP-1 receptor agonists have the potential to reduce blood sugar

levels and promote weight loss. Exenatide, liraglutide, and dulaglutide are examples of GLP-1 receptor agonists.

- SGLT2 inhibitors are a relatively new class of drug that works by inhibiting glucose reabsorption in the kidneys, causing excess glucose to be expelled in the urine. These drugs can help lower blood sugar levels and may also improve blood pressure and weight. Canagliflozin, dapagliflozin, and empagliflozin are examples of SGLT2 inhibitors.

In addition to medication, lifestyle modifications are an integral part of managing type 2 diabetes. A nutritious diet, frequent exercise, and keeping a healthy weight can all help to lower blood sugar levels and reduce the risk of complications.

To build a personalized treatment strategy for type 2 diabetes, it is critical to collaborate closely with a healthcare professional. Treatment may involve a combination of drugs and lifestyle changes, and adjustments may be required as the condition changes over time. Frequent blood sugar testing is also necessary to ensure that therapy is effective and that any potential problems are identified early on. People with type 2 diabetes can live healthy, fulfilling lives with the correct treatment plan and continued maintenance.

To conclude, metformin, sulfonylureas, DPP-4 inhibitors, GLP-1 receptor agonists, and SGLT2 inhibitors are among the drugs available to assist manage type 2 diabetes. Each medicine works differently to assist lower blood sugar levels, and treatment strategies are frequently tailored to individual needs and medical history.

7.1.8 Algorithms Used to Analyze Diabetics

Analytical algorithms can be used to analyze various aspects of diabetes management, including glucose monitoring, insulin dosing, and decision support. Here is a detailed look at how analytical algorithms can be used in each of these areas:

1. Glucose monitoring algorithms: Analytical algorithms can be used to analyze data from continuous glucose monitoring (CGM) devices or blood glucose meters to provide insights into blood sugar control. These algorithms can identify patterns and trends in blood glucose readings, such as the effect of meals, exercise, and medication on blood sugar levels. They can also provide personalized recommendations for optimal blood sugar control, such as adjusting medication doses or modifying diet and exercise habits. Some examples of glucose monitoring algorithms include:
   - Glucose trend analysis algorithms: These algorithms analyze blood glucose readings over time to identify patterns and trends, such as high or low blood sugar levels at certain times of day or after certain meals [10].
   - Insulin sensitivity algorithms: These algorithms use data on blood glucose levels and insulin doses to calculate a person's insulin sensitivity and provide recommendations for insulin dose adjustments.
   - Glucose prediction algorithms: These algorithms use data on blood glucose levels, insulin doses, and other factors to predict future blood sugar levels and provide recommendations for optimal glucose control.

2. Insulin dosing algorithms: Analytical algorithms can also be used to suggest appropriate insulin doses for people with diabetes. These algorithms use data on blood glucose levels, carbohydrate intake, and other factors to provide personalized insulin dose recommendations. Some examples of insulin dosing algorithms include:
   - Correction factor algorithms: These algorithms use a person's insulin sensitivity and current blood glucose level to calculate a correction factor, which is used to adjust insulin doses for high blood sugar levels.
   - Carbohydrate counting algorithms: These algorithms use data on carbohydrate intake to calculate the appropriate insulin dose to cover the carbohydrates consumed in a meal.
   - Closed-loop systems: These systems use glucose monitoring and insulin dosing algorithms to automate insulin delivery and provide optimal blood sugar control.
3. Decision support algorithms: Analytical algorithms can be used to help healthcare providers make decisions about diabetes treatment. These algorithms use machine learning and other techniques to analyze data from multiple sources, such as electronic health records, laboratory tests, and patient-reported outcomes [11]. Some examples of decision support algorithms include:
   - Medication selection algorithms: These algorithms use data on a person's health status, medication history, and other factors to recommend the most appropriate medications for diabetes management.
   - Risk prediction algorithms: These algorithms use data on a person's health status, lifestyle habits, and other factors to predict their risk of developing complications from diabetes, such as kidney disease or heart disease.
   - Personalized treatment algorithms: These algorithms use data on a person's health status, lifestyle habits, and other factors to provide personalized recommendations for diabetes management, such as medication regimens, diet plans, and exercise routines.

   Overall, analytical algorithms can be a powerful tool in diabetes management, providing personalized recommendations and insights that can improve blood sugar control and reduce the risk of complications.

7.1.9 Telemonitoring Evidence-based Analysis for Type 2 Diabetics

Telemonitoring is a rapidly evolving technology that is altering healthcare by providing remote monitoring and management of a wide range of medical disorders. In recent years, telemonitoring technology has made significant strides in the management of T2DM. T2DM is a chronic illness that necessitates regular glucose testing, medication adherence, and lifestyle changes. Telemonitoring, or remote patient monitoring via technology, is being investigated as a potentially beneficial approach for managing type 2 diabetes. Telemonitoring for type 2 diabetics has been studied, and the following evidence-based analyses [12] have been discovered:

- Better glycemic control: Several studies have demonstrated that telemonitoring can improve glycemic control in type 2 diabetic patients. A meta-analysis of 15 randomized controlled studies, for instance, revealed that telemonitoring regimens dramatically reduced HbA1c levels.
- Improved treatment adherence: Telemonitoring has been shown to improve adherence to treatment plans. A meta-analysis of 23 randomized controlled studies found that telemonitoring interventions were associated with improved medication adherence and self-care behaviors.
- Hospitalizations and healthcare expenditures may be reduced: Telemonitoring has the potential to reduce hospitalizations and healthcare costs. A meta-analysis of 19 randomized controlled trials discovered that telemonitoring interventions were associated with fewer hospitalizations and ER visits.
- Increased quality of life: Telemonitoring may improve the quality of life for those with type 2 diabetes. A systematic evaluation of 17 randomized controlled trials revealed that telemonitoring therapies improved quality of life and reduced diabetes-related suffering.

Telemonitoring technology has the ability to improve outcomes in T2DM management by providing real-time feedback, guidance, and coaching. Several technological breakthroughs in T2DM telemonitoring are listed below [12]:

1. Continuous glucose monitoring:

    Continuous Glucose Monitoring (CGM) is a relatively new technology that allows people with type 2 diabetes to monitor their glucose levels in real time. CGM systems detect glucose levels every few minutes using a tiny sensor implanted under the skin. This data can be sent to a healthcare provider, who can use it to change treatment regimens. CGM has been demonstrated to enhance glucose control, decrease hypoglycemia risk, and increase patient satisfaction. Furthermore, certain CGM devices can inform patients when their glucose levels exceed their intended range, offering real-time feedback and support.

2. Wearable technology: Wearable gadgets, such as smartwatches, can track physical activity, heart rate, and other health indicators. These devices can assist people with type 2 diabetes in monitoring their exercise and activity levels, which can have a substantial impact on glucose control. Wearable gadgets can also provide reminders and notifications to assist people with type 2 diabetes stick to their treatment schedules. Furthermore, some wearable devices can provide real-time input on glucose levels, allowing individuals to make informed treatment decisions.

3. Apps for mobile devices: Glucose levels, medication adherence, and diet can all be tracked using mobile applications. These apps can also provide reminders and notifications to help people with type 2 diabetes stay on track with their treatment plans. Gamification techniques are used in several mobile applications to make self-management more engaging and entertaining. Mobile applications have been found in studies to improve glycemic

control and patient satisfaction. Furthermore, some mobile applications can remotely connect individuals with T2DM with healthcare providers, allowing for real-time feedback and support.

4. Telemedicine: Telemedicine entails using videoconferencing and other technology to remotely connect patients with healthcare practitioners. This device can be especially beneficial for those with T2DM who have trouble traveling to medical visits. Telemedicine can be used to monitor glucose levels, educate and assist patients, and modify treatment methods. Telemedicine has been found in studies to enhance glycemic control and lower healthcare expenses. Furthermore, telemedicine can provide persons with T2DM with real-time feedback and support, enhancing their self-management abilities and confidence.

5. Artificial intelligence: Artificial intelligence (AI) is a rapidly growing technology with the potential to transform the way T2DM is handled and treated. AI can be used to find patterns and create therapy recommendations by analyzing huge volumes of data collected from diverse sources, such as glucose monitors and wearable devices. AI algorithms can also be used to anticipate hypoglycemia and other undesirable effects, allowing for early management. Furthermore, AI-based telemonitoring can provide real-time feedback and support to people with T2DM, helping them improve their self-management abilities and confidence.

To conclude, despite the promise of telemonitoring as a helpful tool for managing type 2 diabetes, it is crucial to emphasize that not all studies have consistently demonstrated benefits. Therefore, telemonitoring interventions may not be appropriate or effective for all individuals. Individuals with type 2 diabetes must therefore work closely with their healthcare providers to identify whether telemonitoring is appropriate for them and to receive continuing monitoring and help for managing their disease.

REFERENCES

[1] Trikkalinou, A., Papazafiropoulou, A. K., & Melidonis, A. (2017, April 15). Type 2 Diabetes and Quality of Life. *World Journal of Diabetes*, 8(4), 120–129. doi:10.4239/wjd.v8.i4.120

[2] Olokoba, A. B., Obateru, O. A., & Olokoba, L. B. (n.d.). Type 2 Diabetes Mellitus: A Review of Current Trends. *Oman Medical Journal*, 27(4), 269–273. doi:10.5001/omj.2012.68

[3] Basith Khan, M. A., Hashim, M. J., King, J. K., Govender, R. D., Mustafa, H., & Kaabi, J. A. (n.d.). Epidemiology of Type 2 Diabetes - Global Burden of Disease and Forecasted Trends. *Journal of Epidemiology and Global Health*, 10(1), 107–111. doi:10.2991/jegh.k.191028.001

[4] Wu, Y., Ding, Y., Tanaka, Y., & Zhang, W. (2014, September 6). Risk Factors Contributing to Type 2 Diabetes and Recent Advances in the Treatment and Prevention. *International Journal of Medical Sciences*, 11(11), 1185–1200. doi:10.7150/ijms.10001

[5] Type 2 Diabetes | Adult-Onset Diabetes | MedlinePlus. (2021, May 28). Type 2 Diabetes | Adult-Onset Diabetes | MedlinePlus. https://medlineplus.gov/diabetestype2.html (Accessed on 6 Jan 2023).

[6] Scheen, A., Marre, M., & Thivolet, C. (2020, May 21). Prognostic Factors in Patients with Diabetes Hospitalized for COVID-19: Findings from the CORONADO Study and Other Recent Reports. *Diabetes & Metabolism*, 46(4), 265–271. doi:10.1016/j.diabet.2020.05.008

[7] Sneha, N., & Gangil, T. (2019, February 6). Analysis of Diabetes Mellitus for Early Prediction Using Optimal Features Selection. *Journal of Big Data*, 6(13), 1–19. doi:10.1186/s40537-019-0175-6

[8] Peer, N., Balakrishna, Y., & Durao, S. (2020, May 29). Screening for Type 2 Diabetes Mellitus. *The Cochrane Database of Systematic Reviews*, 2020(5), CD005266. doi:10.1002/14651858.CD005266.pub2

[9] Type 2 Diabetes. (2022, December 12). WebMD. https://www.webmd.com/diabetes/type-2-diabetes

[10] Diabetes Prediction using Machine Learning Algorithms. (2020, February 27). Diabetes Prediction Using Machine Learning Algorithms - ScienceDirect. *Procedia Computer Science*, 165, 292–299. doi:10.1016/j.procs.2020.01.047

[11] Wilkinson, M. J., Nathan, A. G., & Huang, E. S. (n.d.). Personalized Decision Support in Type 2 Diabetes Mellitus: Current Evidence and Future Directions. *Current Diabetes Reports*, 13(2), 205–212. doi:10.1007/s11892-012-0348-6

[12] Andrès, E., Meyer, L., Zulfiqar, A. A., Hajjam, M., Talha, S., Bahougne, T., Ervé, S., Hajjam, J., Doucet, J., Jeandidier, N., & El Hassani, A. H. (n.d.). Telemonitoring in Diabetes: Evolution of Concepts and Technologies, with a Focus on Results of the More Recent Studies. *Journal of Medicine and Life*, 12(3), 203–214. doi:10.25122/jml-2019-0006

8 Intelligent Optimization Unit

8.1 PROPOSED FRAMEWORK

The increase in healthcare cost and risk makes people have a decreased level of quality of care without any considerable improvements. The same has been noticed in most of the rural areas in India. Recent research study shows that the incorporation of technology in healthcare brings down the condition of disease statistics to a reduced state in terms of mortality rate, cost of healthcare, and complications in medical conditions. The advance in information technology has led to an increasing affluence in order to collect various forms of healthcare data [1]. It seems that in this digital world, data has become the integral part of all processes with regard to healthcare data analytics.

Due to this fast progress in medical domain, healthcare institutions are collecting medical data regarding their patients. Understanding the medical data efficiently and exploring the knowledge from it requires advanced analytical and machine-learning techniques in order to transform this data into meaningful patterns, relationship, and associations. The revolution has been started with regard to the extraction of useful information from medical data to make decisions at proper levels. Hence, from this perspective, it is noted that technological incorporation in the field of medical informatics provides valuable information to transform healthcare delivery from a reactive to a proactive concern [2].

From the point of researcher and practitioner perspective, the major challenge in healthcare is interdisciplinary in nature. Also, the field of medical informatics is making various advances in medical field from diverse disciplines such as data processing, database, feature section, machine learning, medical researchers, and healthcare practitioners [3]. With this interdisciplinary nature, in order to add richness to the domain of medicine, also by considering the challenge in order to make significant advances, in this thesis, we have proposed an intelligent optimization unit which encompasses the input as medical data and delivers its output to be the optimal set of features to deliver decisions at proper levels. Another challenge in the healthcare sector is 'Data Privacy' that exists between medical practitioners and computer professionals. The data obtained from medical domain is very sensitive because the medical information corresponding to each individual has to be safeguarded with regard to the medical rules and regulations [4]. Moreover, various processes exist in the medical field to conduct research with voluntary members. Medical practitioners have easy access to medical data because their research is often integrated with their medical practice.

On the other hand, accruing medical data by computer professionals for the research work is not so simple without collaboration of a medical practitioner.

DOI: 10.1201/9781003330189-8

Hence, all of these medical challenges can be accepted only if the protocols, data privacy, and its safeguard measured are followed properly. Upon considering these constraints, medical data have to be collected under the supervision of a registered medical practitioner with regard to all the data attributes collected over the stipulated time period.

Clinical data prediction has become a critical factor with regard to day-to-day healthcare. Though even several prediction models have been deployed in clinical practice, the success of a prediction model lies in the realm of determining the risk factors and their relationship with regard to diagnosis and treatment of disease. In general, clinical prediction and supervised learning models fall into the following three categories:

- Statistical models
- Sophisticated models
- Survival analytics models

All of the above categorized models focus toward the determination of relationship between the feature attributes, with a dependent outcome variable. The success of the model to be developed lies in the fixation of operating parameters and learning factors with the algorithm developed. Also, the success in the deployment of the model depends upon the outcome to be predicted. In addition, survival analytics models are used in predicting the patient's survival time. The context of this thesis lies in the development of a decision support model with the applicability of feature selection and machine-learning techniques, which then fall into a sophisticated model. In addition, statistical evaluation has been made with the applicability of statistical estimators who efficiently determine the feature of set relation, pattern, and its context with regard to the disease. In general, processing data is a multi-stage process. Data capture is the first level process in which the tuples of records are assigned with their corresponding class labels. Then, data pre-processing is made in accordance with the types of data elements such as categorical or continuous. If it is of type categorical, then we will search for the type, whether ordinal, nominal, or binary. Then, the fields of each tuple of record have to be searched for missing value replacement. This should be considered as important because some of the important tuple of records which aids for prediction may be left out due to the missing feature.

Then, based upon the data range and its specification, the values of the data are normalized with regard to the data standardization technique. The following are the various forms of data standardization techniques used for standardizing medical data before the start of the data analysis process.

8.1.1 MIN-MAX NORMALIZATION

In this type of normalization technique, the data corresponding to each tuple of record is scaled up to a smaller specified range most probably [0–1]. It is represented as follows:

$$X_{New} = \left[\frac{X_{old} - Min_{X_{old}}}{Max_{X_{old}} - Min_{X_{old}}} \right] \bullet \left(New_{Max} - New_{Min} \right) + New_{Min} \qquad (8.1)$$

where New_{Min} and New_{Max} are the newly specified minimum and maximum values, respectively.

8.2.2 Z-Score Normalization

In Z-score normalization, the mean value corresponding to the modified value is reduced to zero. It is represented as follows:

$$Z_{score} = \left(\frac{X_i - \mu}{\sigma} \right) \qquad (8.2)$$

where μ is the mean value and σ is the standard deviation.

8.3.3 Normalization by Decimal Scaling

In Decimal scaling, the normalization process transforms the data value to $\{-1 \ 1\}$. It is represented as follows:

$$X_{New} = \frac{X_{old}}{10^N} \qquad (8.3)$$

With this prepared data, the subset of features is selected using attribute selection algorithm. The procedure of feature selection is initiated by swarm intelligence technique. Swarm intelligence algorithms work by the collective behavior with the social interactions to offer insights into meta-heuristics. Swarm intelligence algorithms simulate the coordinated working of many individuals that coordinate with self-organization and distributed control mechanism. The complete framework of the optimization unit is depicted in Figure 8.1.

Some of the common learning systems in swarm intelligence include ant colonies, flocking by birds, animal herds, and fish schools. The working of a classic swarm intelligence algorithmic model will have the following properties:

1. The model encompasses many individuals.
2. The relationship among the individuals is similar.
3. The interaction and association among the individuals are based on a collective behavior, which then exploit the exchange of information through the environment (local information).
4. The global learning behavior of the model is generated by the local interactions of individuals with the environment (global information).

The performance of the swarm intelligence algorithm varies in accordance with the type of medical data used. The effectiveness of incorporation with the swarm intelligence algorithm is made through the operating parameters and learning factors over the set of iterations [5]. The fixation of this parametric value enhances

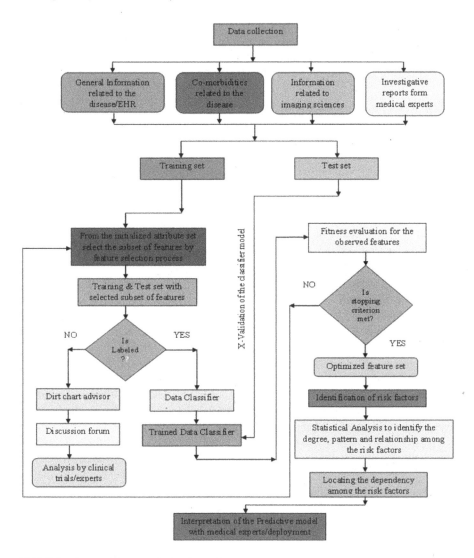

FIGURE 8.1   Intelligent optimization unit.

the performance of the evaluation of the medical data through the fitness function determined by the data classifier [6]. Once this has been done, the data are ready for the training phase which then will be trained by the data classifier [7]. Therefore, the data classifier is responsible for prediction and generalization for future unobserved data points. The classification process is respectively divided into two parts:

- Training model: A data classification component is built from the training model.
- Testing model: The classification part is evaluated and verified on the test model.

- During the training segment, the algorithm has the right to use the values of predicator attributes and the objective attributes equally for all illustrations of the training part, and then it utilizes that information to construct a classification model [8].

This model represents classification information – basically, an association between the predictor attribute values and class labels – that permits the forecast of the class of an illustration given its predictor attribute values. During the testing part, a prediction is made only once and the algorithm is authorized to expose the class label (actual) for the classified scheme. To test the efficacy of the algorithm, a portion of the interpreted data is used to test the algorithm. If the performance of the algorithm is found to be satisfactory, then the machine-learning algorithm can be deployed and assimilated into the rest of the system. Until the stopping criterion is met, the entire phase is iterated and an optimal subset of features is obtained. With the selected set of features, the relationship, patterns, and degree among the risk factors are evaluated through statistical techniques.

The term 'statistics' is defined as the mechanism of representing classified facts ascertaining the conditions of people in a defined state. Those facts can then be stated in a tabulated, visual form of representation illustrating the classified arrangement. In the field of medical science, the statistical tools are used for presentation and analysis of the observed facts that enable the identification of cause and occurrence of disease. Moreover, the efficacy of the model developed can be evaluated by various forms of tests such as T-test, F-test, and analysis of variance (ANOVA). The final phase is the deployment and interpretation of the developed model with medical experts to fix the most notable risk factors that significantly address the locality, likelihood, and nutritional habits of the people.

8.2 DATASET DESCRIPTION

The dataset corresponding to this thesis falls under two categories: one that has been collected from the hospital and the other that has been collected from the repository. The following sub-sections describe the dataset used for evaluating the proposed algorithmic approaches.

8.2.1 BENCHMARK DATA AND ITS DESCRIPTION

Dataset corresponding to four variant diseases has been taken from the UCI machine-learning repository. Datasets corresponding to diseases such as diabetic, heart disease, cancer, and diabetic retinopathy have all been considered for analysis. The Pima Indian Diabetic dataset consists of about 500 tuples of data records with nine attributes in common. The cancer dataset consists of around 600 tuples, each with a class label denoting benign and malignant cancer. There are about nine attributes with a class label signifying the cancer type.

The Diabetic Retinopathy Dataset contains attributes that correspond to the features that are extracted from Messidor image data. This determines the sign of the presence of retinopathy. The dataset consists of 1,150 tuples of records with

20 distributions. Meanwhile, dataset corresponding to heart disease has been observed with 14 attributes including the class label. The class label has five distributions that range from the initial stage of the disease to the final level of transplant. The dataset corresponds to Cleveland clinical foundation containing 303 records.

8.2.2 REAL-WORLD DATA COLLECTED FROM HOSPITALS

Similarly, in addition to the benchmark dataset, a real-world dataset has been collected from a hospital under the supervision of a medical expert, which corresponds to heart disease and type II diabetes. Consecutive CHD subjects of about 306 records were collected from a hospital under a medical expert supervision. The dataset consists of about 24 attributes, with class labels of four categories that correspond to the stages of heart disease. Table 8.1 describes the attributes that correspond to CHD.

The data corresponding to type II diabetes includes 23 attributes, one of which is the class label, as shown in Table 8.2. Each of the attributes has its normal, medium, and high levels of data values that exactly signify the initial level, pre-diabetic condition, and the occurrence of diabetes.

The attribute level varies in accordance with the male and female subjects who are at the stages of diabetic condition [9]. Also, the fixation of attribute levels into various categories is followed as per the Diabetic Association of India and the WHO.

TABLE 8.1

Attribute Description for Heart Disease Data Collected from Hospital

Attribute Name	Description
Age	Age in years
Sex	Sex ($1 = $male; $0 = $female)
Chest pain type	(a) Compressive Type radiated to arm
	(b) Retrosternal area pain
	(c) Pricking type
	(d) Prepetition C chest pain
	(e) Substernal chest pain
	(f) Obstructing chest pain
	(g) Chest pain antennas
	(h) Chest pain with jaw and neck pain
	(i) Pain at Exertion/Sweating
	(j) Pain at rest
	(k) No chest pains
	(l) Constricting pain C
Systolic blood pressure	(1) Normal level ≤ 140 mm/Hg
	(2) Abnormal > 140 mm/Hg
Diastolic blood pressure	(1) Normal level ≤ 90 mm/Hg
	(2) Abnormal > 90 mm/Hg

(Continued)

TABLE 8.1 (*Continued*)
Attribute Description for Heart Disease Data Collected from Hospital

Attribute Name	Description
Serum cholesterol	Level 1 – Desirable (<200)
	Level 2 – Borderline High (200–239)
	Level 3 – High (>240)
Fasting blood sugar	Level 1 – Desirable (<100)
	Level 2 – Impaired Glucose (100–125)
	Level 3 – Diagnosis of Diabetes (≥126)
Restecg	Electrocardiographic result value
Weight	Weight of the corresponding patient in kgs
Waist circumference	(a) Women – (>35 inches)
	(b) Men – (>40 inches)
Smoking	Value – 0 (No)
	Value – 1 (Yes)
Hypertension	It is a cardiac chronic condition
Hypercholesterolemia	Hypercholesterolemia is the presence of high levels of cholesterol in the blood
Previous Angina	İt gets developed at the stage of exertion and gets resolved during rest ,condition
Prior Stroke	Cerebrovascular accident
Anterolateral	Value – 0 (No)
	Value – 1 (Yes)
Anteroseptal	Value – 0 (No)
	Value – 1 (Yes)
Inferolateral	Value – 0 (No)
	Value – 1 (Yes)
Inferoseptal	Value – 0 (No)
	Value – 1 (Yes)
Septo-anterior	Value – 0 (No)
	Value – 1 (Yes)
Diabetes	Value – 0 (No)
	Value – 1 (Yes)
Obesity	Value – 0 (No)
	Value – 1 (Yes)
Family History of CHD	Value – 0 (No)
	Value – 1 (Yes)
Pericardial Effusion	Pericardial effusion is an irregular increase of fluid
Label	Class 0 – Angina, Class 1 – Myocardial Infarction, Class 2 – Percutaneous Coronary Intervention, Class 3 – Coronary Artery Bypass Graft surgery

TABLE 8.2
Attribute Descriptions for Type II Diabetic Data Collected from Hospital

S.No.	Attribute Name	Description
1.	Age	Age of the person
2.	Fasting Plasma Glucose (FPG)	Taken before the consumption of fluids or breakfast
3.	Postprandial Plasma Glucose(PPG)	Taken 1½ hours after the consumption of diet
4.	Glycosylated Hemoglobin(A1c)	To identify average plasma glucose concentration for three months in the human body
5.	Mean Blood Glucose (MBG)	Mean glucose level for three months in mg/dL
6.	Total cholesterol	Below 200 mg/dL would be considered as normal
7.	Triglyceride Level (TGL)	A type of fat which has been determined by food consumption
8.	Low-Density Lipoprotein (LDL) cholesterol	Bad cholesterol deposited over arterial blood vessels
9.	High-Density Lipoprotein (HDL) cholesterol	Good cholesterol which maintains the arteries at an optimal level
10.	Very-Low-Density Lipoprotein (VLDL) cholesterol	VLDL is one-fifth of the triglyceride level, although this is less accurate if the triglyceride level is greater than 400 mg/dL
11.	Non-High-Density Lipoprotein (NHDL) cholesterol	NHDL cholesterol is the total cholesterol minus HDL cholesterol: NHDL cholesterol = Total cholesterol − HDL cholesterol
12.	Blood Urea (BU)	BU test is used to determine how well kidneys are working
13.	Streptokinase (SK)	It is an enzyme test (streptococci)
14.	Albumin Creatinine Ratio (ACR)	The urine albumin test or ACR is used to screen people with diabetes, chronic disorder, and hypertension
15.	Total Protein	Total protein which comprises of albumin and globulin
16.	Albumin	It is an enzyme test (produced in the liver)
17.	Globulin	An enzyme which is responsible for the effective functioning of circulatory system
18.	Serum Glutamic Oxaloacetic Transaminase (SGOT)	An enzyme which is present in liver and heart cells
19.	Serum Glutamic Pyruvic Transaminase (SGPT)	An enzyme which is present in liver and heart cells
20.	Alkaline Phosphatase (ALP) Test	A protein test in blood level found in all tissues

(Continued)

TABLE 8.2 (*Continued*)
Attribute Descriptions for Type II Diabetic Data Collected from Hospital

S.No.	Attribute Name	Description
21.	Gamma-Glutamyl transpeptidase (GGT)	The GGT value measure corresponds to the level of enzyme GGT in blood
22.	Hemo (HB)	The protein red blood cells which carry oxygen from lungs to tissues and bring back carbon dioxide to lungs
23.	Class Label	The label value which depicts the occurrence of the disease

It has been observed from Table 8.1 and Table 8.2 that the significant risk factors for heart disease and type II diabetes are more prone to low, intermediate, and high-level values. If any deviation is noted, it should be measured by the significant test followed by corresponding physician consultation. Also, the risk factors adhering to real-time analysis may vary from time to time based on the symptoms and nature of the disease.

REFERENCES

1. H. A. Heathfield, Jeremy C. Wyatt. (1993). Philosophies for the Design and Development of Clinical Decision-Support Systems. *Methods of Information in Medicine*, 32(1), 1–8. doi:10.1055/S-0038-1634896
2. Frank E. Harrell, Peter A. Margolis, Sandy Gove, Karen E. Mason, E. Kim Mulholland, D. Lehmann, Lulu Muhe, Salvacion Gatchalian, Heinz F. Eichenwald. (2005). Prognostic/Clinical Prediction Models: Development of a Clinical Prediction Model for an Ordinal Outcome: The World Health Organization Multicentre Study of Clinical Signs and Etiological Agents of Pneumonia, Sepsis and Meningitis in Young Infants, 251–286. doi:10.1002/0470023678.CH2B(II)
3. Reinhold, Haux. (2006). Individualization, Globalization and Health--About Sustainable Information Technologies and the Aim of Medical Informatics. *International Journal of Medical Informatics*, 75(12), 795–808. doi:10.1016/J.IJMEDINF.2006.05.045
4. Kenneth W. Goodman. (1999). *Ethics, Computing, and Medicine: Informatics and the Transformation of Health Care.* Kluwer Academic Publishers, Netherlands vol. 1, 303–306.
5. Reiner Horst, Tuy Hoang. (1992). *Global Optimization: Deterministic Approaches.* Springer Berlin, Heidelberg, Springer. ISBN: 978-3-540-61038-0 Published: 11 November 2013, 1–730. doi:10.1007/978-3-662-03199-5
6. James C. Spall, *Introduction to Stochastic Search and Optimization: Estimation, Simulation, and Control*, published: 26 March 2003, Print ISBN: 9780471330523, John Wiley & Sons.
7. David D. Lewis. (1998). Naive (Bayes) at Forty: The Independence Assumption in Information Retrieval. Lecture Notes in Computer Science [Internet]. 1998; 4–15. doi:10.1007/bfb0026666
8. J. R. Quinlan. (1986). Induction of Decision Trees. *Machine Learning*, 1, 81–106.
9 R. David, G. Leslie, Eric S. Kilpatrick. (2009). Translating the A1C Assay Into Estimated Average Glucose Values: Response to Nathan et al. *Diabetes Care*, 32(1), e11. doi:10.2337/DC08-1524

9 Conclusion

This chapter summarizes the research work conducted and its significant outcomes. Also, it points to the future work and its implications. The limitation is also discussed in this chapter. The thesis is concluded with the scope of future research in medical data with technological implication in determining the risk factors related to a specific disease.

In this book, we have proposed the development of a decision support model with the intersection of swarm intelligence and data classification techniques for medical data. The improvement in the development of the model has been made in accordance with the operating parameters and their metric values.

Even though several prediction models exist in clinical practice, the success of the prediction model lies in the realm of the predictive power in determining the risk factors related to specific disease. In this book, a framework (Intelligent Optimization Unit) for clinical data analysis has been proposed which can be explicitly used for evaluating and predicting the risk related to a specific disease with any of the combination of algorithms.

In the first approach, the model has been developed using ACO-DT. In this model, the features are selected using state transition rule and are updated using pheromone update rule. The feature set has been built with features having top pheromone values. The performance of the model shows the accuracy of about 94.6% with 11 features for real-world type II diabetic dataset. From the result, it has been observed that an overall 11 features are high when estimating the performance of the model. Also, this model selects some of the non-important features for both real-world and repository data that are extremely too far in evaluating the risk related to the disease.

In the second approach, the model has been developed using BHS-DT. The BHS algorithm modifies the Memory Consideration rule of the Harmony Search. The implementation results show that the accuracy level estimation for type II diabetic data was found to be 92.87% with a minimum of three features. The model was found to be good for heart disease and benchmark datasets. Also, this model lags in the test interpretation and evaluation among the risk factors.

So, by considering both the factors, from the two models, we have proposed the third model using PSO-DT for clinical data analysis. This model outperforms the mathematical model in the evaluation of medical data for accuracy and features selected with best evaluation for feature correlation, interpretation, and evaluation. The improvement has been made by incorporating self-adaptive inertial weight with modified convergence logic. The correlation among the features has also been found to be perfect with the investigations made by the medical experts. The accuracy of the model with regard to type II diabetic data was found to be 98.60% with four important risk factors. The experimental results for heart disease and benchmark datasets are also found to be improved with this proposed model. The test interpretation and

DOI: 10.1201/9781003330189-9

evaluation was made using Fisher's LDA. The test interpretation results show the ROC value of 0.887 with a significant level of <0.0001.

Hence, nature-inspired computing plays a significant role in disease prediction and classification with medical informatics. Risk factor analysis in medical is a vital problem in recent days. The determination of risk factors with regard to location, likelihood, and dietary habits is the one that is essentially needed by medical experts. This book provides a decision support model to enhance the risk analysis and classification in medical data. The developed model can be efficiently used for risk factor analysis with its comorbidities for a real-world medical problem, which is the major issue identified in the literature.

9.1 SUMMARY OF THE RESEARCH WORK AND ITS SIGNIFICANT OUTCOMES

The research work presents a decision support model using feature selection and data classification with statistical significance. Among the models developed, the proposed model using an improved combination of PSO with Decision trees with statistical evaluation using LDA was found to be extremely good in medical data. Hence, this can be used extensively for region-based analysis of risk factors that contribute to specific NCD. The decision support model developed can be well utilized by the medical experts in two ways:

- It helps them to explore medical issues and key risk factors related to each group of people with respect to their locality, likelihood, and their dietary habits.
- It makes them solve their work practice challenges and utilize the software model in health-related problems and health management, thereby providing people with a 'Valuable Healthcare Service'.

9.1.1 RESEARCH FINDINGS

The aim of this book, as mentioned, is to develop a decision support model for clinical data analysis. The model has been developed using swarm intelligence and data classification techniques with statistical evaluation. A unified Intelligent Optimization Unit has been developed which suits all possible combinations of feature selection and data classification techniques.

This book is focused on the development of the right combination of algorithmic models with improvements in predictive performance and analysis. The first model developed using ACO-DT has no improvements with regard to the number of features selected. During the feature selection process, a measure of feature with the low similarity value is added when selecting the next set of features. Thus, the feature set is sorted in accordance with the similarity measure with the pheromone values. The centralized action is the mechanism to update the global information so as to decide upon the bias during the search process from a non-local perspective. The level of increase or decrease in the level of trial value results in the terminating condition with an improved or reduced level of solution for the given search space.

The model developed using BHS-DT modifies the Memory Consideration rule of the Harmony Search. The Harmony Search exploitation is mainly controlled by HMCR value. The improvement is seen for parametric values, such as HMS = 10, Harmony HMCR = 0.8, PAR = 0.3, and the number of iterations depends on the stopping criterion. The fitness is evaluated using DT algorithm with a ten-fold cross-validation. It has also been found that the age group of greater than 30–50 has a specific impact on the influence of diabetes with respect to the mean glucose level. The PPG level among the influenced people is equal to or above 11.1 mmol/L (200 mg/dL). Hence, from the mathematical model, it is proved that the age, PPG, and MBG levels depend upon another in the determination of diabetic nature of a given patient's health record.

Finally, the PSO-DT model provides the complete analysis with regard to the risk factors related to type II diabetes. There are about two learning factors C_1 and C_2 (cognition and social learning factors) which have to be fixed during the calculation of the fitness function. The values $C_1 = C_2 = 2$, indicating that the social and cognition learning have the same effect on velocity update. Since each of the particles associated with the swarm has inherited variant differences in each state of iteration, it is logical to have self-adaptive inertial weight at the individual level. For the inertial weight of about 0.9, the accuracy is found to be 98.60% with an external calibrated iteration value of six with detailed internal estimates. The observed R^2 values among the correlated attributes 0.5392, 0.5058, 0.4927, and 0.1658 are also found to be significant. Hence, this model can be effectively used to determine the risk that corresponds to a specific disease.

9.1.2 LIMITATIONS

This research completely focuses toward the development of decision support model for medical data that corresponds to NCD. A complete analysis has been made for type II diabetic data and its contributing risk factors. The size of the data and the time taken to evaluate the model can still be improved with its corresponding contributing measures. An effective analysis and model development can be made for the dataset corresponding to communicable diseases and their syndromes with a focus on behavioral risk factors.

9.2 FUTURE WORK

In this book, we have examined the performance of swarm intelligence techniques with data classification paradigms for clinical data analysis. The interpretations of the proposed approach with clinical data show an improvement in predictive power and performance measures. The future work focuses on different combinations of feature selection algorithms and data classification techniques. The improvement can be formulated with the adoption of different combinations of parametric values. Data optimization techniques such as Firefly, Cuttlefish Algorithm, Grey wolf optimizer, and Swallow Swarm Optimization can be adopted since the domain of medical informatics is in need of clinical decision support model with the incorporation of information technology to make decision at proper levels.

With this need analysis, the future community gets benefited by the development of such models with information technology in biomedicine. As a result, the target measure in the determination of the risk factors in accordance with the concerned disease can be known in advance, and the implication of the disease can be prohibited. The nature of location, likelihood, and dietary habits of the patients vary significantly from region to region. Similar to this research work, region-based analysis can be made in accordance with the severity of communicable and non-communicable diseases.

Index